HALF BRAIN FABLES AND FIGS IN PARADISE

Half Brain Fables and Figs in Paradise

JACQUES M. CHEVALIER

The 3-D Mind
Volume One

McGill-Queen's University Press
Montreal & Kingston · London · Ithaca

© McGill-Queen's University Press 2002
ISBN 0-7735-2355-3

Legal deposit third quarter 2002
Bibliothèque nationale du Québec

Printed in Canada on acid-free paper that is 100%
ancient forest free (100% post-consumer recycled)
and processed chlorine free.

This book has been published with the help of a grant
from the Humanities and Social Sciences Federation
of Canada, using funds provided by the Social Sciences
and Humanities Research Council of Canada.

McGill-Queen's University Press acknowledges the
support of the Canada Council for the Arts for our
publishing program and the financial support of the
Government of Canada through the Book Publishing
Industry Development Program (BPIDP).

National Library of Canada Cataloguing
in Publication Data

Chevalier, Jacques M., 1949–
The 3-D mind
Includes bibliographical references and index.
Contents: 1. Half brain fables and figs
in paradise – 2. The corpus and the cortex –
3. Scorpions and the anatomy of time.
ISBN 0-7735-2355-3 (v. 1)
ISBN 0-7735-2357-X (v. 2)
ISBN 0-7735-2359-6 (v. 3)
1. Neuropsychology. 2. Semiotics – Psychological aspects.
3. Semiotics – Philosophy. 4. Psycholinguistics.
5. Language and languages – Philosophy.
6. Neurophysiology. 1. Title.
QP360.5.C43 2002   302.2   C2002-900769-0

Typeset in Sabon 10.5/13
by Caractéra inc., Quebec City

À mes parents qui m'ont appris à penser

Contents

HALF BRAIN FABLES AND FIGS IN PARADISE

Log On: Hyperlinks

What is the mind compared to the brain? What is an idea compared to a word, a picture, a sign? One is "mental" and the other "physical"? One consists in thought and the other is a thing that contains thoughts about things? One is the kernel that hides and the other is the tangible shell or outer covering that does the hiding? But how do we know that thought really exists if it always hides? Has anyone ever seen a thought? Apparently not. Yet many of us have seen images of the brain. We have heard sound images and have seen visual imageries. So why do we hold on to this ghostly entity we call the "mind"? And why speak of the brain as a thing that contains or covers a non-thing? That is, why cast the whole brain in the mould of a "cortex," in the likeness of the bark that covers the inner fibre of human thought?

This book and the two that follow address these intriguing connections between brain, sign, and mind. Tentative answers to the many questions raised by this triad will be found at the intersection of three fields: neuropsychology, semiotics, and philosophy. Studies of how the brain functions from a neuropsychological perspective are examined together with philosophical considerations regarding the workings of language and the sign process. Efforts are also made to show how concepts adapted from neuropsychology and philosophy actually work in concrete symbolic situations. The illustrative material I have chosen for these exercises comes from different sources. In this book, the symbols I explore range from western naming practices to botanical imageries appearing in Genesis (the fig apron motif), English poetry (hemlocks in Longfellow's *Evangeline*), and native Mexican mythology (the Nahua corn myth). Semiotic studies offered in *The 3-D Mind 2* include personal anecdotes, cultural identity rhetoric (debates over Nubaness in Sudan), animal symbolism (frogs and beavers in Canada), body piercing, and foot fetishism (of biblical and pornographic proportions). In *The 3-D Mind 3* connections between brain and sign activities are illustrated through my close reading of a cat drawn by a child, scorpions in Revelation, and ritual prescriptions of heat and cold in Mexican Nahua agriculture.

While apparently eclectic, these analyses have one common goal, which is to shed light on how brain and language interface. Questions raised along the way follow a relatively simple plan reflecting the actual structure of the brain. This book focuses on the lateral aspects, that is, differences and connections between the cognitive functions of right and left hemispheres. This corresponds to the sagittal plane of neuroscience, the plane that dissects brains into right and left halves. The axial plane, which is tackled in *The 3-D Mind 2*, divides the upper and lower parts of brain structures and functions. To this plane corresponds divisions and linkages between the attentions and inhibitions of affect and judgment (normative, instrumental). *The 3-D Mind 3* takes a coronal, frontal, or transverse view of our subject matter. It emphasizes communications between anterior and posterior lobes of the brain and related investments of remembering and planning.

Our journey through *The 3-D Mind* echoes the x, y, z axes of Kinsbourne and Hiscock (1983). That is, "the vertical coordinate (y axis) delineates a progression from the spinal cord to the neocortex, the lateral dimension (x axis) is representative of left-right hemisphere differences in the cerebral cortex, and the z-axis represents an anteroposterior cerebral progression" (see Boliek and Obrzut 1995: 638).

This triad is fundamental to cerebral activity. Accordingly, all fibrous weavings of the brain can fall into one of three categories:

1   commissural neurons linking the two hemispheres;

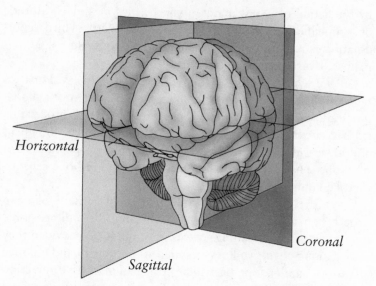

The 3-D brain (2nd ed., Rosenzweig, Leiman, and Breedlove, *Biological Psychology*, 36)

2 projection fibres linking cortical and subcortical structures; and
3 associative connections between anterior and posterior lobes.

Thus "if one starts by thinking of the cortex as a sheet, it is essential to update this conception to accommodate the data concerning pathways, laminae, maps, and columns. With increasing degrees of accuracy we can think of the cortex as a *stack* of sheets, then as a stack of *sheets with methodical vertical connections*, then as a stack of sheets, *some of which are topographically mapped*, with methodical vertical connections, and finally, *as containing cells with highly specific origins and projections*" (Churchland 1986: 137). These are living fibres that permit movement in thought, language, and space.

Motions of the brain could be mapped on to those of flying. In order to take off and move through the air, birds and flying machines must work on three planes simultaneously. First, movements are generated along the lateral axis, with wings occasionally tipping to the right or the left if necessary. Second, these actions are synchronized with vertical movement obtained by the action of wings maintaining the bird at a given altitude or propelling the body upward or downward. Third, coordination is required along the longitudinal axis, the plane that regulates variations in speed and direction.

On the whole, the brain follows similar principles. For it to take off and follow a determinate route, it must mix (1) adequate allocations of right and left brain cognitive processing; (2) a contextually specific balance of upper-cortical judgment and lower-subcortical affect; and (3) a correct proportioning of rear-lobe sensori-associative processing and front-lobe sensori-motor planning.

Given that language is a product of brain activity, one can expect sign activity to be cast in the same three-dimensional mould. Signs and meanings can be set in motion provided they evolve along cognitive lines, respond to normative and emotive attentions, and adopt particular forms of narrative direction and speed. The resulting weavings point to reticles of neural communications and meanings in language. The reticulum is the supporting structure of nervous tissue, also known as neuroglia (neuro-, and Gr. *glia*, glue). It consists of a special type of branched cells that binds together and supports the nervous tissue of the central nervous system. More generally, a reticle, from the Latin word *rete*, a net, denotes a network of fine lines. This is precisely what the sign process consists of: the constant spinning of a finely meshed network of lines and interstices, with lines crisscrossing each other in multifarious directions.

The philosophical implications of this overview of brain and sign activity are many. Among other things it means that theories of language and signification that give priority to either logic (structuralism), norm (functionalism), reason (positivism), emotion (psychoanalysis), or narration (hermeneutics) are all useful and incomplete at the same time. Each theoretical position offers a partial view of the complex phenomenon it is supposed to address.

A critical issue that follows directly from this three-dimensional mapping of brain and sign activity revolves around the age-old question of order versus chaos. When looking at weavings of neurons and signs, should we not give priority to chaos over order – to rhizomes over the orderly branching of axes and disciplines? Is it not the case that the brain is so complex and sign activity so shifting and sliding that no serious generalization can be made as to how they actually operate? Should we not let the rule of relativity reign over phenomena that are utterly fractal? That is, should we not endorse the Heraclitean attitude generally prevailing in poststructural semiotics and postmodern philosophy? To use Heraclitean language, should we not let the primary element of fire reduce all absolutes to ashes, laying all essences and regularities to rest in the graveyard of western metaphysics? Should we not let scientific regularities or appearances thereof yield to the eternal flux and restlessness of all things?

Some will be inclined to reject the Heraclitean attitude and choose instead to give credit to science where credit is due. They will then opt to take advantage of advances in neuropsychology and extend our understanding of brain activity to studies of sign processing. But if they do so, they will be well advised not to trespass on preserves occupied by the humanities and the social sciences. Neuroscientists who attempt to exhaust the subject matter of semiotics will soon be invited to abide by the long-standing principles of modesty and open-mindedness that should prevail in the natural sciences. After all, good scientific practice is never imperialistic. Hard science assumes rather that any phenomenon we look at is part of a complex reality that can never be fully comprehended. This requires disciplinary focusing, as in normal neuroscience, the kind that puts everything in a paradigmatic perspective but does not require philosophical completeness. No theoretical frame worthy of science should ever be so dogmatic and comprehensive as to aim at eliminating other disciplines. Grand efforts to reach a synthesis of brain and sign activity from a neuroscientific perspective are therefore suspect from the start. This warning will meet with even greater approval amongst students of the humanities and the human sciences. More than anyone else, they will be suspicious of neuroscientific temptations to occupy semiotic and philosophical territorialities not under the purview of the natural sciences. When reading neurology into symbolism or culture, prudence is in order; brain studies gone imperialistic are synonymous with neurobiological reductionism!

These comments bring us back to a difficult choice imposed by current debates pertaining to our subject matter: opting between the human and the natural sciences, between the soft wisdom of field-dependent relativism and the hard findings of nature-grounded realism. In this book and others that follow, I choose not to choose. More positively, I opt for a dialogue between modes of knowledge that have drifted apart over the centuries and continue to ignore one another with bewildering stubbornness. In one corner, we have hard scientific views on brain structures and functions. In the other, we have the contributions of humanities, social sciences, and philosophy to studies of language and culture. In the analyses to follow I give priority to dialogical exchanges between these exclusive contributions to studies of brain and sign activity. To be more accurate, my preference goes to a postdialogical strategy: developing a transdisciplinary perspective that cuts across fields of knowledge and schools of thought, towards a "subject matter" that is neither brain nor mind, strictly speaking, but rather indistinguishably both. The perspective in question starts with the assumption that distinctions between mind and brain no longer make sense. The question is whether or not they ever did.

This postdialogical endeavour is not an easy path to follow. Attempts to build bridges across fields of knowledge require that recognizances into each territory be done with rigour and a good grasp of current states of the art. Accordingly, the exigencies of disciplinary scholarship are reflected in the structure adopted throughout my essays in neurosemiotics. Each book proceeds methodically from neuropsychology to illustrative semiotics and philosophical afterthoughts. This overall plan, however, entails certain costs. For one thing, it shows dependence vis-à-vis the boundaries I wish to overcome, reproducing disciplinary partitions otherwise critiqued. Just as I address neuropsychological issues in their own terms, so too my semiotic analyses and philosophical considerations should stand on their own. Proceeding otherwise would be foolish. Inventing each field from scratch is neither feasible nor useful. Contributions to their crossbreeding cannot be done at the expense of advances made in each domain.

All the same, this book and the others that follow take up the difficult task of exploring overlaps and hyperlinks between neuroscience, semiotics, and philosophy. While this does not preclude further specialization and conceptual fine-tuning within each field, the basic premise adopted here is that key concepts used in the human sciences are not and need not be qualitatively different from terms used and applied in the natural sciences. Note that the argument goes both ways: there is no self-evident reason that sign production and neural activity should be studied in isolation from one another. More than ever, theoretical modelling permitting fertilization across these fields is possible and long overdue. Thus we shall see that signification and neural communication converge on a middle ground phenomenon consisting of "nervous sign" activity, a mode of processing that is physical and meaningful all at once.

A postdialogical blending of neuroscience and the humanities can be applied to all three levels of brain and sign processing. On the lateral plane (*The 3-D Mind 1*), issues pertaining to right- and left-brain thinking can be linked to semiotic assemblages of similarities and differences. While couched in different languages, those of half-brain talk and theories of the "Code," the two approaches to cognitive activity are treading similar paths. On the vertical plane (*The 3-D Mind 2*), theories of instrumental reason or the unconscious seen from a Habermasian or Freudian perspective stand to benefit from research on prefrontal brain activity and LeDoux's emotional brain, and vice versa. The longitudinal dimension should also be revisited in a transdisciplinary perspective. In *The 3-D Mind 3*, I argue that neuropsychological studies of memory and planning activities can inspire and take inspiration from Derridean considerations about *différance*, Heidegger's conception of being-in-time, and the Ricœurian hermeneutics of narrative movement.

Cratylus Returns

This book calls two notions into question: first, the notion that we must attend to either the objective-physical or the subjective-mental aspects of sign activity; and second, the idea that we must choose between universals in nature (e.g., brain mechanisms) and fractals in culture (e.g., the polysemic evocations of metaphor). In hindsight we might say that this twofold dilemma concerning the particular and universal, subjective and objective aspects of language has been with us for a very long time. Actually it goes back to the dialogue pitting Socrates against Cratylus, a philosophical text written by Plato more than 2,300 years ago. In this dialogue Plato portrays Cratylus as a defender of Heraclitean becoming. Cratylus contends that signs of language are fixed through the whims of cultural conventions and arbitrary associations between words, ideas, and things. Socrates takes the opposite view. Word assemblages are grounded in the true nature of things and reflect permanent essences. Signs are *and should be* copies of what they signify.

A close reading of this dialogue sheds light on issues we are still grappling with. Socrates tries to convince Cratylus that names are not given simply by whim, custom, or taste. Rather, they are assigned on the basis of proper connections with reality. For instance, Oreste is "the man of the mountain," a name designed to signify the brutality, fierceness, and wildness of this hero's true nature. The word *soma* is another good example, one that is particularly relevant to our critique of signs and the brain viewed as shells or containers holding ideas, kernels of truth, or essences of the mind. The word *soma* denotes indeed the body and is a natural match for what it means. In the words of Socrates, "some say that the body is the grave [*sema*] of the soul which may be thought to be buried in our present life; or again the index of the soul, because the soul gives indications to (*semainei*) the body; probably the Orphic poets were the inventors of the name, and they were under the impression that the soul is suffering the punishment of sin, and that the body is an enclosure or prison in which the soul is incarcerated, kept safe [*soma, sozetai*], as the name *ooma* implies, until the penalty is paid; according to this view, not even a letter of the word need be changed." But if this word is a natural match for what it means, how is it that the term is not found in all languages? Socrates admits that words other than *soma* can be used to signify the body. But his contention is that while letters, sounds, and syllables may vary, the forms and meanings intended can remain the same. Thus "the etymologist is not put out by the addition or transposition or subtraction of a letter or two, or indeed by the change of all the letters, for this need not interfere with the meaning," says Socrates.

Socrates views naming as an instrument naturally adapted to the work it does, which is to teach us the essences of things. It acts like a shuttle that disengages the warp from the woof. Words demarcate the nature of beings in the same way that a shuttle distinguishes threads in a web. The weaving metaphor is somewhat surprising as it implies an assemblage of threads and lines, as opposed to immutable elements independent from one another. Yet it aptly evokes Socrates's conception of naming, that is, an instrument that imitates through assemblages of original elements. Assemblages of sounds and words in language allow essences to be properly understood through combinations of relevant origins and component meanings. The true nature of a thing can thus be understood by delving into connections between words and their origins and also between component parts forming sentences.

But there is a problem, says Socrates. Origins have origins of their own that may be lost, and component parts such as words in a sentence may be further unpacked into syllables and sounds. So where does the search for true meaning stop? Whence did the phonetic *s-o-m-a* assemblage come to mean the body or grave in the first place? Socrates's answer to this question lies in primary elements that cannot be further decomposed. Letters and syllables fulfil this function. They are like the notes and colours that musicians and painters use to imitate whatever it is that music and painting are designed to copy. For instance, the sound *r* is obtained through an agitation of the tongue and becomes an excellent instrument for the expression of motion and rapidity (as in roe, trembling, striking, etc.).

There is another problem, a riddle that concerns the moral aspects of Socratic epistemology. Is the teaching function of naming something that "essentially is" or something that is ethically desirable? Is Socrates reflecting on what *must be* in the sense of *what is*, or are his "teachings" to be understood in the sense of what *should be*? Is naming descriptive or pre-scriptive? The answer lies somewhere in between. In Cratylus, the question as to what names actually do is inseparable from considerations about what they should be doing. In order to do the teaching it is meant to, an instrument that weaves names to things must be designed correctly (by the legislator) and must be used properly (by the dialectician). But errors in naming can be made, and the instrument can go wrong. Some names may not fit designated things. For instance, names given to heroes or humans can be deceptive. Some are simply inherited from ancestors. Others may be exercises in wishful thinking (e.g., Eutychides, the son of good fortune).

But how do we know that a naming error has been made? Socrates finds the solution to this puzzle in the knowledge of things acquired through means other than names. Knowledge obtained through naming is subject to errors that can be assessed through independent means. Things and their nature can be known independently of words used to signify them and cannot be altered by names. In the final analysis direct knowledge of essences and things studied in themselves is the nobler and clearer path to truth. Knowing beyond words (and thinking before speaking) is the only standard by which the rightness or wrongness of verbal assemblages and imitations can be assessed in the first place.

According to Socrates, a telling example of wrongful naming can be found in all names that rely on principles of motion and flux to capture the permanent essence of a particular virtue or divinity. Chronos and Rhea are two good examples of this. The word for "name" (*onoma*) is another instance of a word misrepresenting the true nature of a thing. If properly chosen, the word *onoma* should capture the essence of the noun or naming instrument itself, which is to teach things by means of words made in the natural likeness of things to be named and taught. But the word for "name" fails to do that. Instead of designating that which clearly captures the essence of a thing, it connotes the action of seeking, "signifying *on ou zetema* (being for which there is a search); as is still more obvious in *onomaston* (notable), which states in so many words that real existence is that for which there is a seeking (*on ou masma*); *aletheia* is also an agglomeration of *theia ale* (divine wandering), implying the divine motion of existence." A word denoting the fluid nature of things in motion is wrongfully applied to a stable tool essentially meant to capture fixed essences. The name-givers responsible for this confusion fall into the Heraclitean trap of imposing unhealthy notions of "natural restlessness" on to the nature of language. In doing so they deny and undermine the foundations of true knowledge. They lead others to believe "that all things leak like a pot, or imagine that the world is a man who has a running at the nose."

Socrates mentions *pseudos* as another naming instrument that misrepresents the true nature of things. Since it stands for falsehood, the term should evoke motion and instability. Instead, *pseudos* means stability and evokes signs of sleep-like stagnation and forced inaction. According to this name, things deemed to be false are things that do not move. The word is a derogatory misrepresentation of the permanent, the stable, and the universal. It confounds falsehood with immutability, the source of all truth.

Names should be suited to the things they name. But Socrates goes on to say that even when reproducing their qualities in language, words can never be the exact counterpart or perfect double of what they are designed to represent. Otherwise who could tell the difference between a name and what is named, hence between word and world? Imperfections in language are thus to be expected. This not to say that words are fated to lose the general character or essence of what is being said. Names can still succeed in being truthful, provided they contain some degree of resemblance to the essences they signify.

Much to Socrates's credit, the story ends without a forceful conclusion. Cratylus is not convinced by the teachings of Socrates and continues to prefer the views of Heraclitus. *Noblesse oblige*, Socrates is dialectical enough to invite his attentive friend to come back another day with teachings of his own. Likewise, Cratylus invites Socrates to give further thought to the matter at hand.

Invitations to do more thinking about language, knowledge, and reality have not fallen into deaf ears. The debate was to last for more than 2,000 years. But to no avail. We are now entering a new millennium, and no resolution can be seen on the horizon. Things and thoughts are still viewed as radically separate beasts. The present-day tendency for studies of sign activity to branch out into semiotics (a plurality of fields in its own right) and neuropsychology is not particularly promising in this regard. By and large battles of mutual indifference pit neuroscience against theories of semiotic anarchy. The bifurcation speaks volumes about our persistence in separating not only subject from matter but also fractals in culture from universals in nature. The implication is that there can be no field of investigation located somewhere in the middle of things and thoughts. A "subject matter" consisting of nervous sign activity is begging to be explored.

Brain and sign studies are light-years away from taking each other seriously. The prevailing opinion is that neurons are neurons and signs are signs. Both can be found in the same head, but who knows why we should bother to look at how

the two intersect! Given this declaration of reciprocal independence, efforts to talk about brain and sign activities in a single
breath generate some rather curious claims. Some still hold on
to the bizarre notion that ideas and meanings are like souls
buried in soma-like bodies and bark-like brains. Others continue to claim that ideas and meanings can be delivered through
somatized sign-mailing systems; sound images are letter-like
messages signifying concepts or objects that do no communication of their own. Most sign theorists are now fashionably
critical of this representational doxa, yet they continue to proceed as if sign weavings could be grasped without lessons from
and for studies of neuropsychology.

All is as if we were still stuck with a Judeo-Christian perspective on the body acting as a container of vital forces otherwise immaterial and ghostly. Not enough attention is given
to the fact that neuroscience erodes "the metaphysical convic-
tion that one's *self* is an affair apart from that mound of biological stuff hidden under the skull" (Churchland 1986: 69).
In semiotics and philosophy the simple fact that motions of
thought and body are inseparable tends to go unnoticed. In the
words of Churchland, "even in cases where cognitive deficits
are particularly prominent, there are typically accompanying
motor deficits. This, together with evolutionary considerations
and neurophysiological data concerning how much of the brain
is, in one way or another, implicated in motor control, should
invite us to question any assumption that takes the brain to be
chiefly a device for knowledge acquisition and only incidentally
a device for sensorimotor control" (ibid.: 222).

Neurosemiotics is a modest attempt to move out of these
mind/matter debates and explore whatever may lie beyond,
using building blocks borrowed from many fields. It calls into
question the ignorance generally prevailing in neuropsychology
with regards to whatever semiotics and philosophy may have to
say about culture and language. But it also challenges the current philosophical tendency to reject all claims to universalism
and what follows from this tendency – what Lyotard (1988: xiii,
13) calls a miserable slackening and proliferation of theories

bent on proclaiming a new-this, a new-that, a post-this and a post-that. From monumental theories and doctrines that prom-ised a firm resolution and litigation of all imaginable differences (organized into grand systems and structures), we have moved into theories and doctrines that discover chasms in all nooks and crannies of a "chaosmos" gone frantically postmodern.

Trendy theories of sign rhizomes and fractals are a case in point. They are reminiscent of the bramblescape approach to brain activity: "An impression common outside of neuroscience is that in their organization, nervous systems resemble nothing so much as an endless, untended bramblescape – foreboding, hopelessly tangled, and defiantly intractable. Accordingly, on the bramblescape theory of brain design, figuring out how the brain works is a faintly ludicrous business, since there are too many neurons, too many branches, too many thorns" (Churchland 1986: 99). Whether applied to neurons or signs, theories of absolute restlessness are terminally naive. They are a reminder of the Heraclitean position adopted by Cratylus in the age-old debate pitting mutability against immutability. Views that are less partisan are needed to challenge this bicephalous constitu-tion of our mind/brain, a dual spirit torn between the rigidity of being and the fluidity of becoming.

Churchland (ibid.: 5) confirms that "philosophy has tended to ignore developments in the neurosciences and pretty much to go its own way. Likewise, research in the neurosciences has pro-ceeded without much heed to what philosophers had to say about the nature of knowledge or of mental states. Quite simply, neither found the other useful, and the two disciplines have had largely independent histories. Contact was made only seldom, and then it usually consisted in desultory sparring of the 'mind-body problem'." An interesting exception to this rule can be found in the well-known dialogue between Luria and Jakobson concerning the mutually beneficial insights of neuropsychology and linguistics. In the words of Jakobson (1985: 177), exchanges between the two fields can "open ever deeper insights both into the structure of language with reference to the brain and into the structure of the brain with the help of language." It is true that both disciplines have moved beyond premises of cognitivism and the logic of the intellect or Chomskian Code. Also distinctions between the two specializations need not be as clearcut as they used to be. Students of nervous sign activity can nonetheless find inspiration in these formative efforts at breaking the great wall separating the natural sciences from humanities and the social sciences.

Admittedly, many scientists and philosophers have struggled with questions that concern the relationship between the mental and the physical. Those who are critical of the notion that signs can be coordinated to pre-existing things and ideas are now many. Gadamer, a close reader of Cratylus, argues for instance that words are not hooked up to the mental and the real *ex post facto* with variable success, as Socrates would have it. But Gadamer also objects to the notion that things and the world are created or constructed by language *ex nihilo*. Signs cannot precede all meaningful existence of the real. Rather, "we seek the right word – i.e., the word that really belongs to the thing – so that in it the thing comes into language" (Gadamer 1994: 417). To the extent that word and world are allowed to interact, Gadamer is on the right track. Several questions must nonetheless be answered. Is language any less material than all those things it speaks to? What does it mean for a word to "belong" to a thing? And if things do exist, do they necessarily have to be thought or spoken of as "things"? Couldn't this language of thingness be just what it is, a *construction in its own right*? Why force things to come into language as "things"?

Answers to these questions can perhaps be found in new modes of investigation that simply bracket all familiar distinctions between thoughts and things and signs in between to connect them. Fresh queries that hook up neuropsychology to semiotics and philosophy may be useful in this regard. But the task is formidable. It requires that we understand how the brain intervenes in many forms of sign activity. It also requires that we consider how theories of signification can help us rethink the brain, using a novel language that may undermine "braintalk" as we currently know it. But what language would that be?

The preceding comments imply that thought and mind can be reduced to brain on one condition: that the brain "becomes subject," through art, science, and philosophy (Deleuze and Guattari 1994: 210). Husserl (1965: 154) was right in this regard: the human sciences cannot and should not try to be exact. A better question, however, is whether any science should aspire to exactitude. The question applies to brain studies. Can they succeed where philosophical speculations about the mind have failed? Can neuroscience objectify the brain? I think not. As Deleuze and Guattari (1994: 209) put it, "it seems difficult to treat philosophy, art, and even science as 'mental objects,' simple assemblages of neurons in the objectified brain ... If the mental objects of philosophy, art, and science ... have a place, it will be in the deepest of the synaptic fissures, in the hiatuses, intervals, and meantimes of a nonobjectifiable brain, in a place where to go in search of them will be to create."

But what does this "nonobjectifiable brain" look like? Doesn't the sign process add up to organic connections of the neurological and chemical sort? Who will deny that signs are products of the brain? This author would not. Granted that this is true, however, there are critical choices in language to be made. What words shall we use to make sense of this "sign neurochemistry"? Whatever words we use, will they not constitute one discursive "reticle" at best, just one finely meshed construction within an infinitely large array of images and signs that are virtually infinite and that are bound to go beyond the language of neuron and synapse? In the end neurons can never be addressed without reference to other things that they are not and that are bound to impact on brain and sign activity. Neuropsychology can never be disconnected from other discursive treatments of "thought, mind and brain," treatments ranging from art to philosophy and even theology.

Signs that speak specifically of the brain are inevitably embedded in broader constructions and weavings of the brain. Given these entanglements, our "nervous sign system" approach to brain and sign tissues will necessarily entail a conceptual network developed right in the middle of the multiple, apparently conflicting theories of neurons, language, and mind. In keeping with this, what I am aiming at is not a comprehensive approach to the "subject matter" at hand. Any contribution to brain and sign activity is bound to evolve in a context involving larger surroundings, with influences and inputs inevitably coming from and heading "elsewhere." Our nervous sign system paradigm has therefore as much chance of capturing the full powers of brain and sign activity as consciousness has in grasping the unconscious and the body (Deleuze 1988: 18). As with neurons and signs, all theories "do not begin to live except in the middle" (Deleuze and Parnet 1987: 55). While neurosemiotics is an exploration of brain and sign activity, it pursues not the transcendental construction of a "brain behind the brain but, first of all, a state of survey without distance, at ground level, a self-survey that no chasm, fold, or hiatus escapes" (Deleuze and Guattari 1994: 210).

Readers will have understood by now that neuroscience is my starting point for a rethinking of semiosis, mental activity, and philosophy itself. This is in keeping with what Derrida (1973: 94; 1981a: 34–6) has to say about mathematics, a statement that applies even better to neuropsychology. Like all sciences, both disciplines imply a far-reaching protest against metaphysics. Mathematics does so through nonphonetic inscriptions involving interrelated notations that produce meaning without object representation (the number 26 speaks to other numbers, not to any object). Sign numbers preclude all denotative or indicative contaminations involving personal pronouns and proper names. They are freed from all space- and time-specific adverbs such as "here" and "now" and related specifications of the *hic et nun*. As Socrates remarks in his dialogue with Cratylus, the slightest alteration changes the actual meaning of numbers; words used to "represent" these numbers are established by artificial convention or custom alone, not through representation by likeness. All in all, numbers are word-sign connectors that do not abide by the natural similarity theorem, a cornerstone of western representational metaphysics (Gadamer 1994: 406, 412–18, 428–43).

In my view, however, neuropsychology is far more challenging than mathematics. It calls metaphysics into question by undermining all conceptions of an abstract mind dwelling in crannies and crevices of the brain. Having said this, the riddles of semiosis will not let themselves be deciphered through neuropsychology or mathematics, let alone a "formal" marriage between the two. After all, both sciences partake in the Leibnizian pursuit of laws of universal simplicity and constancy, a quest for the secular spirit inhabiting the body and the world we live in. This is the modern version of Logos, a logic that recycles God into a mind hiding through sign-manifestations of itself. When in contact with brain studies, philosophy may have to be renewed, yet the same should be said of neuroscience: given its emphasis on the complex weavings of brain activity, it too must accept locating itself in a larger web. At stake here is a multilayered approach that does justice to the complexity and sophistication of language and that avoids simple mechanisms "prescribed in the wax of the brain" (Derrida 1973: 141). Like grammatology, studies of the nervous sign process must both mark and loosen the limits of classical scienticity.

But knowing the limits of neuroscience is no excuse for not doing a good "survey without distance, at ground level" of the field in question. To this task we now turn, with particular reference to the findings and assumptions of half-brain talk.

THE NEURAL WEB

Half Brain Talk

There is considerable evidence from neuropsychology that each hemisphere of the human brain shows distinct cognitive preferences or advantages. The literature that we are about to review, however, is not without problems. For one thing, hemispheric modelling tends to be done at some cost to our understanding of complementarities and integrative connections between the two hemispheres. Another problem lies in the language and terminology commonly used to capture differences between right and left hemispheres (RH, LH). While some hemispheric specialization can hardly be denied, students of neuropsychology have no easy task when using words to characterize the proclivities of each brain let alone processes to integrate them. On the whole, bipolar terminologies currently adopted may not be simple and flexible enough to characterize the building blocks of brain activity. They are not simple enough in that they tend to be insufficiently detached from activities (e.g., auditory and visual processing) that are so complex as to require bihemispheric input. They also lack in degrees of conceptual flexibility or cultural freedom; that is, more often than not, they are closely tied to wholesale theories of the "mind" derived from western philosophical history.

The fact that the two brains are differentiated in structural, functional, and biochemical terms is generally known. Though they are interconnected, hemispheres are structurally demarcated by the longitudinal fissure. Morphologically, the left side is larger and shows more intricate foldings (Iaccino 1993: 5–8).

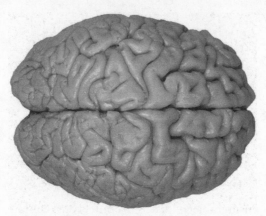

The two hemispheres (viewed from above).
(Sundsten, *The Digital Anatomist*)

The language-related *temporal planum* region, which includes much of the Wernicke area, is usually larger on the left side, especially among children and right-handed subjects. The observation holds true for about two-thirds of the normal population. Cases of either symmetry or reversed asymmetry, however, do not necessarily result in linguistic deficiencies (Hynd et al. 1995: 631). The differences between the two halves are functional in that each hemisphere specializes in certain physiological tasks. Each controls the opposite side of the body via a crossing of the nerve pathways. The right brain controls the use of the left limbs, while right-limb use and dominance is generally governed by the left hemisphere.[1]

But the right and left hemispheres also show different ways of gathering and organizing knowledge. Studies of hemispheric differences launched by John H. Jackson more than a century ago and resurrected in recent decades by Orstein (1977) and others provide us with ample evidence of the cognitive aspects of brain lateralization. There is now a vast literature suggesting that the verbal brain, usually the left, is auditive, analytic, sequential, and motive. By contrast, the non-verbal hemisphere, usually the right, is visual, holistic, spatial, and emotive. The fact that the right brain functions holistically means that it applies intuition and synthesis to knowledge of the world, using a simultaneous-gestalt mode of information processing.

The notion that each hemisphere works differently at the cognitive level is verified in neuropathological studies of brain injuries and diseases. Experimental methods have also been used to confirm this phenomenon of hemispheric specialization. They include standard dichotic and tachistoscopic procedures. Dichotic listening tests consist in presenting sounds to each ear with the use of earphones. Tachistoscopic procedures involve verbal or non-verbal material presented for very brief moments to either the right or left visual fields, with the subject fixating on a central point. Both tests are used to explore differences in how each hemisphere processes information received contralaterally; input into the right ear or eye activates the LH, whereas input into the left ear or eye feeds into the RH. Other standard experimental methods include body side movements (e.g., eye movements, facial expressions), metabolic indices (e.g., cerebral blood flow, positron emission tomography), and brain wave analyses (e.g., electroencephalograms).

The notion that cerebral hemispheres possess different cognitive styles is generally accepted. The actual ways in which these differences are to be characterized are still being debated and raise important issues about the language generated by scientific minds to speak about everyone's brain.

THE LEFT HEMISPHERE: VERBAL, AUDITIVE, ANALYTIC, TEMPORAL (DIACHRONIC), AND MOTIVE

Consider the job description assigned to our left brain. To begin with, the LH is usually portrayed as having special abilities in processing the input and output of linguistic material. This is confirmed by half-field tests involving digits, letters, syllables, and words. This verbal material may be sensical or non-sensical and can be spoken dichotically. Results show that utterances are heard and processed differently or unevenly by each ear. For instance, different consonant-vowels and complex tones

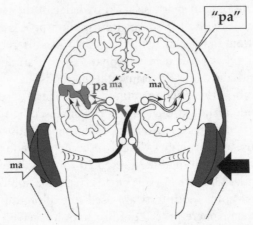

Kimura's model of the right-ear advantage. When conflicting information
goes to both ears, that to the right ear reaches Wernicke's area first.
The subject repeats only the right ear information. (Rosenzweig, Leiman,
and Breedlove, *Biological Psychology*, 542)

presented simultaneously to each ear result in right- and left-
ear advantages of 5 per cent to 15 per cent, respectively.[2] The
left side of the brain is thus more responsive to the phonological
or acoustic aspects of language (especially consonants), as
opposed to mere tones. Eye and head movements associated
with word spellings, définitions, and simple arithmetic show an
LH advantage as well (Iaccino 1993: 126; Bruder 1995: 662).
Tests using verbal or non-verbal material can also be administered tachistoscopically, with a view to probing these LH advantages. Since these tests are visual by nature, however, they tend
to be less revealing of special connections between language
and the LH.

Readers should bear in mind that language lateralization
on the left side does not apply to right-handed people only.
While the vast majority of right-handed people show a left-brain
dominance for speech (95 per cent), sound (80 per cent), and
visual stimuli (70 per cent), the corresponding figure for left-
handed and ambidextrous subjects is also high (69 per cent for
speech; see Iaccino 1993: 60; Peters 1995: 199; Churchland 1986:

197). Some of those who have developed unusual right-brain language capabilities may have done so due to early LH damage. Many of them are "pathological left handers" who show a variety of disorders that are not necessarily caused by their left-handedness (Temple 1993: 101).

Poor performance on verbal tests is a typical symptom of LH damage. Injuries to this side of the brain and experiments of hemispheric paralysis induced through Wada's injection of short-acting sodium amytal technique will result in language disorders or speech impairment known as aphasia (Iaccino 1993: 60). Studies of these disorders date back to the pioneering works of the anthropologist Paul Broca (1824–1880) followed by those of Wernicke (1848–1905). Although global aphasia may be caused by damage involving a broad area of the LH, we now know that different kinds of aphasia can result from lesions or diseases affecting distinct areas of the LH. Cases of aphasia involving right-brain lesions are less than 10 per cent.

Aphasic disorders may entail deficits in comprehension, a faulty processing of linguistic input usually stemming from left-rear hemispheric problems. Symptoms include Wernicke's aphasia, where messages heard or read are poorly understood. Words are used inappropriately or jargonistically, producing neologisms and paraphasic substitutions such as "cake" for "bread" or "curl" for "girl." Pure verbal auditory agnosia can occur as well. This is when familiar words are no longer recognized. Colour agnosia, the inability to recognize verbal representations of colours, may also result from lesions to the left posterior cortex.

Cases of Wernicke's aphasia typically involve insults to posterior regions of the left superior temporal gyrus (as in word deafness) and neighbouring parts of the parietal cortex such as the supramarginal and angular gyri (as in word blindness). The angular gyrus is particularly important as it links the auditory and visual regions. It permits conversions of auditory forms into visual patterns, hence words heard into their corresponding spelling. According to disconnection theory (see Rosenzweig et al. 1999: 532), damages to connections between

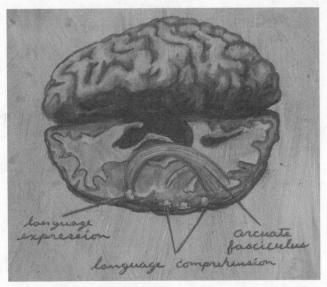

The *arcuate fasciculus* transmits information between
Wernicke's area and Broca's area (drawing by Martin Blanchet)

auditory and visual areas may be at the origin of writing problems known as alexia.

By contrast, Broca's motor or nonfluent aphasia entails difficulties in the processing of linguistic output. Symptoms can take
the shape of expressive-motor articulation problems or speech
impairment, usually with a partial paralysis of the right side of
the body. Tasks affected include repeating verbal messages,
naming persons or objects (anomia), and writing. Subjects may
have a hard time constructing grammatically correct phrases and
sentences using verbs and function words. Automatic speech
(e.g., swearing, greeting expressions) may be left intact. Language production problems typical of Broca's aphasia are often
associated with injuries to the low-rear section of the left frontal
lobe (especially the third frontal gyrus and neighbouring lower-
end regions of the motor cortex). Unlike Wernicke's aphasics,
these patients show awareness of their difficulties.

Conduction aphasia should be mentioned here. It consists in
paraphasic errors (using sounds or words other than those
intended) combined with marked repetition and word-retrieving

deficits. Speech remains relatively fluent and word comprehension intact. This appears to be caused by lesions to the *arcuate fasciculus* in the left inferior parietal lobe, neural pathways that connect Broca's and Wernicke's language areas. More will be said in *The 3-D Mind 3* on the role of these anterioposterior connections within each hemisphere.

Another clinical confirmation of an LH linguistic disposition comes from studies of split-brain subjects. Verbal stimuli presented dichotically to these commissurotomized subjects reveal a near extinction of left-ear information. Because not primarily connected to the LH, the left ear (stimulating the RH) is less efficient at registering information of a verbal nature. In normal subjects, linguistic stimuli coming in through the left ear and RH can be passed on from the right side to the left side of the brain through interhemispheric connections. Split-brain patients, however, cannot compensate the auditive weaknesses of the RH by counting on a callosal transfer of information (Hugdahl 1995: 126).

Autistics are known to display left-brain language problems, possibly due to a delayed acquisition of specialized left-brain language skills. A greater proportion of autistics are left-handed compared to non-clinical populations, which suggests a preferred right-brain cognitive style.

Other clinical symptoms of LH disorder include stuttering and dyslexia, especially among left-handed males (Iaccino 1993: 107). While dyslexia involves different subtypes and is a fuzzy clinical category, the most common syndrome is of a phonological nature. Deep dyslexia thus refers to subjects who tend to focus on meaning, an RH concern, at the expense of details pertaining to precise categorization, sound, or spelling. The subjects experience an auditory-linguistic, LH deficit. Words belonging to the same semantic fields are used interchangeably; for instance, the word "table" becomes "chair" when read out loud. Abstract and nonsense words are difficult to read since meanings are not easily recognized.

The LH is good at processing fine distinctions in sounds, letters, and digits. In keeping with this, it works analytically, breaking reality into discernible parts or features. This is to say that the left brain focuses on details and differences as opposed to similarities and configurations. It captures the defining aspects or qualities of perceived objects and allows us to categorize what we see with relative precision. For instance, imaging the lower-case version of upper-case letters entails an act of discrimination that the left brain will perform with greater effectiveness compared to the other hemisphere. A similar left-brain advantage is obtained when subjects are asked to discern a single feature that differentiates two virtually identical test faces (Iaccino 1993: 36, 113).

When the left brain is impaired, patients can reproduce the global pattern but not the local information. For instance, they cannot perceive the small "w" letter distributed in a larger M-shaped configuration, shown below, which they can see

```
W                       W
W  W              W  W
W     W     W     W
W           W           W
W                       W
W                       W
W                       W
```

(Zaidel 1983: 101). The RH can always fill in this gap but does so with limitations. Deep dyslexia also confirms our LH preoccupations with local information, i.e., precise speech utterances, in this case. Right-brain reading allows the left-lesioned subject to understand what is read and even recognize words that are familiar and easily imageable, but not to read the word aloud, especially if the word is unfamiliar, a non-word, or an abstract word with few semantic associations. Or the subject doing RH reading may fail to distinguish the word from closely related semes. The word "chair" is thus pronounced instead of "table" (this a case of semantic *paralexia*); in the absence of an intact left-brain discriminatory function, semantic associations typical of right-brain activity interfere in the act of speaking, with the result that one four-legged piece of furniture is substituted for another (Iaccino 1993: 64). As Temple remarks (1993: 161), it is as if the subject is "reading with a semantic reading system in the absence of a phonological reading system." The lexical reading route is preferred over the phonological. Other indices of impaired left-brain reading abilities include a tendency to drop grammatical endings ("reading" becomes "read") and to substitute short grammatical words for each other ("in" becomes "to," "he" becomes "us," etc.).

The LH assesses and establishes differences on the temporal level as well, emphasizing successive moments in the order of time. It employs a sequential, serial, or diachronic logic and is sensitive to the fact that some sounds, words, images, and actions must come before and others after. This perception and production of patterns of linear succession ties in with a left-brain sensitivity to grammar. When applied to speaking, a left-brain activity *par excellence*, the awareness of time is essential to the sequencing of sounds and signs and the use of proper syntax. This is true even when the phonological aspects of language are discounted; left-lesioned deaf people are likely to run into grammatical difficulties when expressing themselves through American Sign Language grammar. In short, left brain damage interferes with the perception and comprehension of phenomena pertaining to the dimension of time.

Given its responsiveness to sequentiality, the LH specializes in processing information involving duration and also connections between causes and effects deployed over time. It is therefore well equipped to oversee motive activity, hence monitor the planning of motor action, be it verbal or physical. As first argued by Hugo Liepmann in 1900 (see Harrington 1995: 20), the left brain regulates the motions of speech and purposeful movements of the body. The motor function of the LH tallies with the fact that the right side of the body tends to initiate most manual activities and that right-hand dominance is observed among 92 per cent of the population; there are no major cultural differences in this regard (handedness statistics are highly sensitive to definitional classifications and measurements, however;

see Peters 1995: 190). Thus left-brain injury is often at the origin of apraxis. This can take many forms, from problems in imitating common gestures to difficulties in putting a command into voluntary action (ideomotor apraxis, e.g., "brush your teeth") and organizing and performing a sequence of learned acts (ideational apraxis) (Iaccino 1993: 63). Constructional apraxis is another possible effect of a left brain injury (the parietal lobe); the subject can draw an overall configuration but will leave significant details and features out of the drawing.

In short, the LH is verbal, auditive, analytic, temporal (diachronic), and motive. Recent developments in neuropsychology, however, have shown that some of these hemispheric attributions are more problematical than was originally thought. Also, the complexity of interhemispheric connections is such that we must be careful not to assign fully fledged cognitive activities to each hemisphere. All indications are that the brain can do few things only using one hemisphere at a time. More shall be said about these important qualifications later.

THE RIGHT HEMISPHERE: NON-VERBAL, VISUAL, HOLISTIC, SPATIAL (SYNCHRONIC), AND EMOTIVE

Unlike the left brain, the RH functions non-verbally and holistically. It specializes in a gestalt mode of information processing, emphasizing visuality, spatiality, simultaneity, and emotivity. This is the hemisphere that grasps synchronic forms, figures, and orderly patterns that cannot be broken into discernible features, be they parts in space or moments in time.

The visual-holistic brain is particularly active when subjects are shown simple non-verbal stimuli presented tachistoscopically (dot displays, line orientations, etc.), or simple configurations such as wholes, blobs, or schematic models of classes of objects. Tests that consistently show an RH advantage involve drawing, doing jigsaws and puzzles, assembling blocks, manipulating geometric figures, or matching parts to the whole. The right brain is also good at constructing configurations from missing elements or incomplete patterns, an operation known as *completion* or *stimulus closure*. The same hemispheric preference is obtained when subjects are asked to match objects they touch with both hands with visual images presented simultaneously or afterwards. Compared to sequential tasks, simultaneous matchings tend to yield stronger RH (left-hand) superiorities. Split-brain subjects will also make more use of this gestalt hemisphere when matching parts to the whole. This is especially true if tactile experience and free-form shapes are involved, as opposed to visual discriminations and complex structural arrangements requiring greater left brain involvement (Iaccino 1993: 34, 78).

Given the holistic, spatial, and tactile ("hands-on") dispositions of the RH, subjects suffering from lesions to this side of the brain may have problems converting two-dimensional representations into three-dimensional configurations. They may experience disorientation problems, blindness to the left spatial side (i.e., left hemispatial inattention), or visuospatial impairments affecting hand movements (ibid.: 25, 56). Right-brain learning disorders also include discalculalia, the inability to distinguish objects based on length, shape, amount, or size. Mention should also be made of the non-verbal perceptual-organization-output disability (NPOOD), with such symptoms as visuospatial difficulties, depression, and social withdrawal (ibid.: 104–7). To this list can be added the right-brain impairment version of constructional apraxis: the subject can draw detailed features of a figure correctly but without reconstructing the overall configuration.

We have seen that language is predominantly a left-brain activity. This is confirmed by the fact that reading and reading-comprehension disabilities (alexia) are more frequent among children with left- or mixed-handedness relative to right-handed children. Yet the gestalt brain plays a crucial role in linguistic tasks such as reading. This means that both brains are needed when reading. Dyslexia thus occurs with unusual frequency among children showing signs of one-sided lateralization, which consists in a tendency for most stimuli to be processed by one hemisphere only, be it the left or right side (Boliek and

Obrzut 1995: 650–1). Reading difficulties are not necessarily caused by a neurological deviation or "minimal brain dysfunction." Indications are that they nonetheless entail uneven patterns of neuropsychological organization involving *a neglect of either right or left hemispheric functions* (Hynd et al. 1995: 618; Boliek and Obrzut 1995: 645).

As already noted, when the left brain is neglected, deep dyslexia may result. Surface dyslexia (also known as visual-spatial, semantic, or RH dyslexia) is what happens when the opposite scenario occurs. This is when reading is done principally by the LH, without the full contribution of the right brain. When reading, surface dyslexics focus on letter-sound connections pronounced in proper sequence. They can convert letters into the sounds forming a word and have therefore no difficulty reading nonsense and abstract words. The fact that surface dyslexia children have a good mastery of rules of correspondence between letters and sounds means they generally perform better at school compared to children with deep dyslexia. Surfaced dyslexia patients nonetheless experience real problems as they cannot reassemble component parts into a meaningful gestalt. They find it hard to read homophones and words that have irregular spelling. Impaired readers will thus fail to process the contextual-gestalt information required to strike a choice between homophones (is it "sail" or "sale"?). Also they will make mistakes when converting words with irregular spelling into correct sound pronunciations (is it "ough" as in "dough" or as in "rough"?) (Iaccino 1993: 97; Temple 1993: 183). All of these problems are symptomatic of a left-brain tendency to focus on details as opposed to looking for meanings in context.

Another advantage that the right brain derives from its synthetic abilities is the leading role it plays in the process of identification and the perception of "near-identities" based on relations of similarity. A right-brain advantage is thus obtained when testing procedures involve recognizing photographed faces and schematic facial drawings, or selecting faces that closely match split face representations (chimeric figures with two different facial halves fused into one). Injuries or tumours affecting the RH (inferior temporal lobe and region bordering the parietal lobe) may result in agnosia, an impaired ability in identifying people or familiar faces (prosopagnosia), objects, and locations. These patients also "show diminished spontaneity in conversation, hesitation and blocking in finding the right word, and difficulty in giving definitions and paraphrases" (Churchland 1986: 188).

The right brain is preferentially equipped to use language with emotive intent and to comprehend symbols and humour, wit, *double entendre*, and innuendo. In keeping with these findings, right-brain damage can cause patients to display inappropriate affective responses. The same patients may experience difficulties in interpreting contextual cues, connotative and analogical meanings, metaphors, stories, sarcasm, jokes, and cartoons (Liotti and Tucker 1995: 393). A right-parietal lobe injury can also cause dream impairment, which tallies with the importance of symbolic activity in dreams.

While not specialized in phonetic processing, the gestalt brain is good at connecting sounds or words with the contextual information needed to make sense of a given communication, be it verbal or written. Insults to the right temporal lobe can thus lead to difficulties in recognizing environmental noises through familiar contextual associations (Temple 1993: 48). The information derived from emotive circumstances is particularly important in this regard. The RH is highly sensitive to contextual signs and expressions of accent, mood, prosody, and emotional tone. When judging the mood of chimeric faces, right-handed subjects will typically show an RH bias and focus therefore on the face appearing in the left visual field. Also, the left side of the face (activated by the RH) is usually perceived as showing more intense emotionality compared to the right side (ibid.: 197, 199). Clinical studies have shown that lesions to the RH (anterior lobe) can be expected to affect the capacity to express oneself with intonation, making one's speech rather flat; this is known as affective aphasia. Alternatively, right-brain damage (posterior lobe) can reduce the subject's ability to identify the tone of language used by others, or the face picture illustrating a particular tone of voice described verbally (Iaccino 1993: 62). Aphasic and RH patients have also been reported to show more difficulty in reading or recalling emotional words and stories (Liotti and Tucker 1995: 392). Another well-documented sequel of a right-brain injury is the loss of musical ability, known as amusia, a loss of tonal memory and the consciousness of melodic patterns, loudness, and associated timbre (Iaccino 1993: 35).

The holistic mode attends to the emotional, spatial, and parallel-configurational aspects of reality. It pays less attention to factors of seriality or time-dependent sequentiality. Eye and head movements associated with emotional inquiries, musical recognitions, visualizations, and spatial assignments confirm the right-brain advantage in non-analytic areas of human brain activity. Correlatively, the RH appears to be relatively more active in emotionally related situations of implicit learning, dreaming, and altered states of consciousness. While accessible to RH-lesioned patients, "unaware learning" or autonomic classical conditioning involving emotional circumstances is more dependent on the RH than on the left. In the words of Hugdahl, "associative learning to emotionally relevant conditional stimuli are represented in the right hemisphere, particularly for negative, aversive stimuli" (Hugdahl 1995: 261). This hemisphere also plays a key role when the whole brain is at sleep and in a state of dreaming, generating stories where past and future exist side by side and chronology is without meaning (Iaccino 1993: 33–5). Lastly, in keeping with this sleeptime activity, RH dominance is observed when subjects experience altered states of consciousness (Hugdahl 1995: 241).

Two Brains Are Better Than One

Studies of split-brain subjects confirm generalizations regarding the cerebral lateralization phenomenon. Subjects who have undergone split-brain surgery show right-brain spatial responses to stimulations presented on the left side of the body. An RH preference is also obtained when non-verbal, manipulospatial responses are solicited: for example, pointing to a picture among a series of alternatives (Iaccino 1993: 75).[3] Likewise, patients will use their left hand or RH body language (giggling, blushing) to identify or respond to left field objects or images (nude pictures). They do so without showing LH verbal awareness of them; language cannot be accessed when stimulation comes from the left visual field.[4] Nor will verbal instructions (understood by the LH) to move or write with the left hand be accomplished with facility, if at all (Temple 1993: 67–8). Conversely, LH verbalizations are given in response to right-hand movements or stimulations presented in the right field. Subjects can name (an LH operation) only those objects, letters, or images appearing to their right. If the word "hemisphere" is flashed centrally on a screen, they will report seeing the right-field word "sphere" alone.

All of these experiments suggest that when the two hemispheres are separated, appropriate verbal and non-verbal responses cannot be generated simultaneously. The two cognitive modes act independently of one another and can even lead to conflicting actions; for instance, one hand unbuttoning a shirt and the other hand trying to button it, or each hand selecting a different dress to wear. Facial expressions of emotions (RH) will be poorly verbalized (LH), and verbal expressions will not necessarily be reflected in facial expressions (Iaccino 1993: 23, 72–3).

Let's say a split-brain patient is shown a snow scene on the left side and a chicken claw on the right hand side and is asked to pick from an array of pictures something that matches each scene. The left hand is then likely to pick, say, a shovel and the right hand, say, a chicken head. But what if the patient is asked to explain the connection between these two choices, using left-brain language to make sense of the shovel/chicken-head assemblage? One possible answer is that the chicken claw goes with the chicken and a shovel is needed to clean out the chicken shed (see Churchland 1986: 190). Interestingly, there is no consciousness of a split choice process. The subject *speaks* as if the two conflicting choices were integrated into a single logical scheme controlled by the verbal brain (LH).

Another good illustration of differences in hemispheric cognitive strategy is obtained when commissurotomized subjects are asked to match objects together. If a cake image is projected to the LH, the metonymic, functionally related "spoon and fork" option is chosen. But when projected to the RH, then the similarly shaped hat figure is preferred; in other words, the appearance match takes precedence over the function match.

Unlike split-brain patients, normal subjects use both hemispheres simultaneously. The implication is that commissurotomy may not be the best laboratory for analyses of hemispheric activity. Although extremely valuable, research on split-brain patients tends to approach the brain from a specialization perspective, to the detriment of how we understand processes of interhemispheric communication. If lateral specialization occurs at all, it is by virtue of the functional interaction and complementarity that can develop between the hemispheres. Communication and complementarity between the two hemispheres are all the more important as most of the cognitive activities humans engage in are of such high-order complexity that two brains will always be better than one. Each hemisphere may be better at

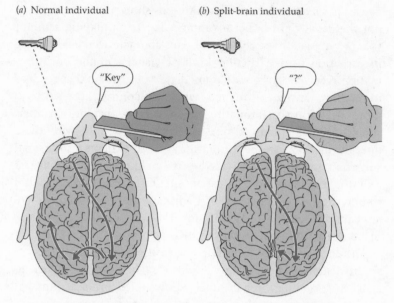

(a) Normal individual   (b) Split-brain individual

Testing of a split-brain individual. (Rosenzweig, Leiman, and Breedlove, *Biological Psychology*, 540)

performing certain tasks, yet the complementary role of the other half should not be underestimated. As Sergent (1995: 158) argues, "the modularity of the brain is embedded within a highly *interactive* nervous system."

Visual operations apparently regulated by the RH may serve to illustrate the integrative functioning of the brain and the intersection of cognitive functions in the simplest activities. The right brain is commonly thought to specialize in perceptions of spatiality. All the same, visuospatial actions such as drawing objects on command or copying line drawings require LH input. As Iaccino notes (1993: 10), these are composite activities that can hardly be engaged in without detailed, analytic information processing. Complex wholes can be reconstructed only if the parts are adequately recognized.

One test that confirms this left-brain contribution to spatial comprehension is the discrimination of tachistoscopic targets, a task that may under certain conditions show an LH superiority, not the usual right-brain advantage. Far from playing a minor role in visual activity, the LH is better characterized as directing its attention to a particular kind of visual stimulation: information received from one's immediate "peripersonal space," as in reading, writing, or manual work. By contrast, the RH pays more attention to stimulation received from distant, extrapersonal space (Heilman 1995: 229–30). In keeping with these finer distinctions, studies of brain-damaged patients and normal subjects tested through divided visual field experiments suggest that the LH tends to "focus on smaller parts, higher spatial frequencies, or details ... in contrast, the right hemisphere appears to focus on the global form, lower spatial frequencies, or course patterns" (Brown and Kosslyn 1995: 78).

Although typically associated with the RH, music is also a sophisticated, whole-brain activity. Perfect pitch (involving exact note naming), for instance, shows a left-brain advantage. Also, given their temporal organization, intricate tonal arrangements and rapidly changing acoustic patterns will entail left-brain activity, which is responsive to the linear aspects of music – sequential ordering, duration, and rhythm. When subjects are exposed to elaborate musical sequences presented dichotically (using earphones), bihemispheric involvement is thus observed. Also, the analytic and temporal intricacies of music are such that a left-brain advantage is observed amongst knowledgeable listeners exposed to tests involving melodic presentations.

The rule of bihemispheric complementarity applies also to predominantly left-brain activities such as speaking, writing, and reading. These linguistic tasks require right-brain processing, as confirmed by studies of blood flow to the RH during language-related activities (Temple 1993: 98). This is no surprise, given that the production and comprehension of language requires input from the RH and its ability to apprehend form, context, and meaning. As already pointed out, studies of surface dyslexia confirm the importance of right-brain involvement in reading and reading comprehension. Studies also show that the right brain performs better when reading material is presented not in standard typescript but rather in handwriting or some spatially complex formats: for instance, Gothic typescript, Kanji Japanese characters, mirror-oriented letters and digits, or Braille characters (Iaccino 1993: 112–14, 119). The right-ear, left-brain advantage reported in many studies of auditory processing does not preclude right-brain involvement either. As Hugdahl (1995: 151) points out, "the right hemisphere is not a passive 'slave,' acting only as a relay station for the left ear signal. As data from both normals and brain-lesioned patients have shown, the right hemisphere does process the left ear stimulus to some degree, even when the stimulus is a cv [consonant-vowel] syllable."

That the RH is heavily involved in linguistic operations is confirmed by research on split-brain patients. Like other subjects, commissurotomy patients show signs of hemispheric specialization: given the absence of LH input, the RH seems linguistically impaired. As with nominal aphasics, their disconnected right brains can thus identify the use and basic qualities of an object presented in the left visual field but not its specific name. With the exception of some single-word clichés or phrases, muteness of phonological impairment is the rule. Nor can split-brain subjects associate faces with particular names. However, they are capable of some coordination between movement and language. They can execute manipulospatial instructions presented orally (e.g., arranging differently coloured plastic shapes viewed by one hemisphere alone), as long as the verbal directions remain simple. They can match spoken words with left-field images and their written counterparts, provided that the words are concrete and familiar, hence well-engraved in the subject's verbal memory. Moreover, split-brain subjects can execute some limited left-hand writing, they can comprehend simple grammar and syntax, and they can grasp visual word gestalts (as opposed to elaborate textual meanings) (Iaccino 1993: 79–80; Zaidel 1983). In short, the RH seems capable of some linguistic understanding. This is so true that without these right-brain supplementary language skills, disconnected left brains have a much harder time performing linguistic tasks and show symptoms of reduced vocabulary and reading speed.

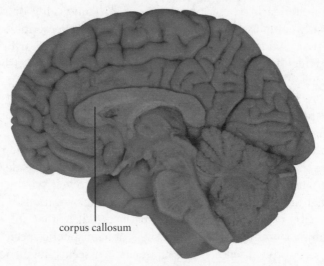

corpus callosum

The corpus callosum (Sundsten, *The Digital Anatomist*)

We may conclude from these findings that hemispheric differences involve flexible and complementary processing modes
rather than absolute asymmetries (Iaccino 1993: 127, 136).
While specializing in certain cognitive tasks, each hemisphere
assists the other in producing composite brain activity. As in
music and language, bihemispheric coordination may be the
rule, not the exception. All in all, "the left hemisphere is more
language oriented than the right, whereas the right is more visuospatial oriented than the left. Although relatively specialized for
a particular input, each hemisphere still requires the other to
complement its overall functioning" (Iaccino 1993: 10).

When the whole brain is engaged in elaborate cognitive activity, cerebral blood flow measurements point to a balanced
involvement of both hemispheres. In the case of normal subjects, coordination and integration of the two hemispheres are
both performed through nerve fibres connecting mirror-image
points of lobes on each side of the brain. Interhemispheric
pathways include multiple channels of the corpus callosum.
These commissural channels display different levels of myelin-
ization (fatty sheathing of nerve fibres) and corresponding

variations in functions (e.g., visual vs. motor channels) and transmission speeds. Although internally differentiated, the corpus callosum specializes in transmitting information about identities and spatial positions; subcortical commissures seem better equipped to transmit information about attributes, categories, and emotions (Banich 1995: 429). Some cognitive problems may result not so much from lesions on one particular side of the brain but rather from injuries to these callosal pathways connecting the two sides. For instance, there is evidence to suggest that damage to interhemispheric nerve fibres connecting the language areas to RH visual processing areas may be responsible for visual object agnosia (affecting subjects who can draw or describe an object but cannot name or identify it). Bilateral integration difficulties seem also to be involved in prosopagnosia problems. Recognizing faces is a bihemispheric operation that requires relaying both "the most salient features and holistic configurations of stimuli that have been apprehended many times in the organism's past" (Iaccino 1993: 66).

This brings us to Sergent's analysis of bihemispheric contributions to face-processing activities. Although apparently simple, the recognition of specific individuals following the perception of a face involves several tasks. They include:

- the decoding of gender, age, race, and emotion;
- the perception of configurational features ("physiognomic invariants");
- the acknowledgment of familiarity or unfamiliarity; and
- the retrieval of stored facial representations, biographic memories, and name information (Sergent 1995: 164).

Some prosopagnosia patients fail to perform all of these tasks. Others show a deficit in some face-recognition functions but not others. Could these variable symptoms of prosopagnosia reflect the fact that face recognition requires multiple inputs from the two hemispheres, as opposed to relying on the right brain only? Recent studies in this field point to an affirmative answer. There is reason to believe that "different tasks on facial representations may therefore entail the recruitment of different brain regions" (ibid.: 168). The RH may perform better in the initial storage of facial information. The two hemispheres, however, show equal efficiency in accessing facial information that is permanently stored, as confirmed by study of split-brain patients' facial processing competence. "Whereas unilateral brain damage produces face-processing impairment nearly exclusively after right hemisphere lesion, evidence from split-brain and hemispherectomized patients suggests that there may be functional equivalence of the two hemispheres with respect to the processing of faces or, at least, that destruction of areas in both hemispheres is necessary to produce a complete inability to process faces" (ibid.: 171).

Lesions to the right temporal lobe may block access to biographic memories associated with a name or a face, whereas damages to the left anterior lobe will usually account for name-finding difficulties (ibid.: 176). The left brain is good at assigning a name to a face but is ill-equipped to extract the physiognomic invariants of a face. If disconnected from the RH, it will have problems extending the constant features of a face to different or new views of the same face. Some studies suggest that prosopagnosia (involving whole faces but some object categories as well) is caused in reality by lesions in both hemispheres, typically in areas where the temporal, parietal, and occipital lobes meet (see Rosenzweig et al. 1999: 549).

In the end, bihemispheric integration may be indispensable to most normal tasks. But if so, how can split-brain (often epileptic) patients function at all, which they do? We know from Levy (1974) that despite the cognitive problems they face, split-brain subjects are cognitively functional and appear to have visual perceptions of the world based on integrated gestalt forms. This is confirmed through partial field input tests where each hemisphere receives either one-half of a geometric figure or unrelated halves of a facial picture.

In the absence of two intact hemispheres, a single hemisphere can in some cases fulfil all major cognitive functions with efficiency (Sergent 1995: 161). This presupposes a certain amount

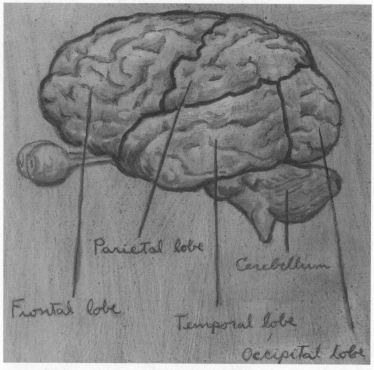

Brain lobes (drawing by Martin Blanchet)

of functional hemispheric plasticity. Thus patients can partially overcome split-brain apraxia problems (performing purposeful actions) by relying on the relative flexibility of each hemisphere. We know that the RH of split-brain patients can recover some expressive speech functions, especially if there is extensive damage to the LH. Left-brain aphasias can also be compensated by right-brain relearning, using language recovery techniques such as singing or melodic intonation therapy (Boliek and Obrzut 1995: 638; Rosenzweig et al. 1999: 535). Recovery is more frequent among subjects who have suffered brain damage before the age of six to eight years, and even more among those who were less than two years old at the time of the injury. Recovery of right-brain functions by the uninjured left brain has also been reported (Iaccino 1993: 57, 67–9; Hynd et al.

1995: 619). Other indices of hemispheric neuroplasticity have been obtained from non-clinical observations of complex hand movements such as typing or finely tuned bimanual movements involving the playing of string instruments.

Hemispheres, however, are not so flexible that lateralization can be said to develop only progressively, thereby playing a relatively small role in children's brains. As Hiscock and Kinsbourne (1995: 548, 551–4) explain, studies of limitations of right-brain language in children have disproved the equipotentiality and progressive lateralization doctrines held true by neurology for a century, a doctrine propounded by Orton in 1928 and popularized by Lenneberg in the 1960s. Other evidence of early lateralization can be found in reports of mathematical difficulties among left-lesioned children, or studies of temperamental problems (mood and rhythmicity) among children who have undergone right hemispherectomy. Mention should also be made of asymmetric postures and preponderant right-side orienting movements in infancy, which suggest an early dominance of left brain activity. Infants respond to adult speech utterances only when looking to the right side. Infants' capacity to hold objects in their right hand (LH) is also greater compared to their left hands. The asymmetric tonic neck reflex (ATNR) is particularly revealing in this regard. In the first month of their lives infants will turn their heads to the right side most of the time, with right limbs extended and left limbs flexed, a position that predispose children to coordinate their gaze with right hand movements.

In short, "human brain asymmetries arise much earlier in ontogeny than previously believed. Both structural and functional differences between the left and right sides of the brain are present at birth, if not earlier. The early emergence of behavioral asymmetries, and the character of the asymmetries themselves, imply that a subcortical mechanism underlies infantile lateralization" (Hiscock and Kinsbourne 1995: 563).

While brain lateralization cannot be denied, hemispheres communicate directly with one another and show some degree of plasticity. The principle of neuroplasticity applies not only to each hemisphere but also to mechanisms of interhemispheric communication. Thus indirect integrative mechanisms can be developed to compensate for the losses incurred through commissurotomy. More precisely, the brain can circumvent the absence of interhemispheric pathways in one of three ways:

1 processing sensorial information through same-sided (ipsilateral) motor connections;
2 employing left-side limbs to respond to verbal commands presented to the LH; and
3 using right-side limbs to act on visuospatial instructions (drawing, block assembly) conveyed to the RH.

To this list should be added cross-cueing as another indirect means of interhemispheric communication. Normally, information exchange is done through nerve fibres of the corpus callosum. Verbal material received and registered by the RH is communicated to the language areas of the LH through the callosum. In the case of split-brain subjects, however, cross-cueing or indirect "cross-talk" between disconnected hemispheres can act as a compensatory mechanism. For instance, when asked to identify a red light, a number, or a face projected in their left field (RH), split-brain subjects may hear themselves giving an erroneous verbal identification generated by their own LH. They can then detect their own facial reaction, left-hand movements, and other signs of body language expressing disapproval or some relevant information related to the object. Given these nonverbal indices of disapproval, they can look for a new answer that will meet with LH approval. Subvocal cross-cueing in the other direction has also been observed. Affective information transmitted from one hemisphere to another through intact brain stem connections can also help subjects improve their responses to tasks requiring bimodal cognitive operations (Iaccino 1993: 80–2).

Given these substitute operations, individuals born without a callosum (a condition known as *callosal agenesis* or prenatal commissurotomy) may resemble normal subjects. While experiencing performance deficits echoing all the problems faced by split-brain patients, they can resort to cross-cueing, ipsilateral pathways, and other interhemispheric pathways (e.g., the anterior commissure) to compensate for the lack of callosal connectivity.

Does this mean that two separate hemispheres doing indirect cross-talk are as good as one integrated brain? Not really. Problems faced by split-brain patients are real. Some of these cognitive limitations have already been discussed. Also, some tests will simply fail to detect the difficulties suffered by these subjects. For instance, face-recognition tests applied to split-brain patients tend to emphasize many trials with repetitions of the same facial viewpoint. These procedures leave out one particular expression of prosopagnosia: the subjects' ability to recognize constant facial features throughout different or new views of the same face. The corpus callosum seems important after all!

UNEVEN HEMISPHERIC SPECIALIZATION

Information appearing in either the visual or the auditory field is processed by the whole brain. Interhemispheric integration involving relatively equal participation of the two hemispheres is typically obtained in complex activities consisting of multiple steps or distinct tasks performed simultaneously and with proper callosal coordination (Banich 1995: 433–8).

Hemispheric specialization nonetheless occurs, and there are three different ways to account for how this actually occurs:

1 Particular signals coming from one half field may be conveyed to the opposite-side hemisphere (e.g., verbal stimuli entering the right ear and going to the LH) through contralateral nerve connections, which appear to be stronger than ipsilateral tracts. Through cross-side connections, each hemisphere captures and processes the information suited to its cognitive mode. Same-side, uncrossed tracts generate less cortical activity, they have fewer fibres, and they may be suppressed when contralateral pathways are activated. Readers are also reminded that without the callosum, dichotic listening

tests reveals a near-extinction of left-ear information (Hugdahl 1995: 126).

2 Provided there is no competing dichotic information coming from the opposite side, ipsilateral tracts may carry the kind of information that the same-side hemisphere is qualified to process. For instance, some left-field verbal material will enter the left ear and feed directly into the LH, thereby reinforcing the left brain's tendency to specialize in verbal tasks.

3 If transmitted to the inappropriate hemisphere through same-side or cross-side pathways, information can always be relayed to the other hemisphere through the corpus callosum. When this happens, however, the information is passed on at some cost, with some deterioration or distortion. "Interhemispheric transmission is a very time-consuming process, as is revealed by simple response time tasks" (Wittling 1995: 339).

The end result is always the same: each hemisphere ends up showing an advantage when performing its preferred tasks. As one hemisphere takes the lead, the other remains active but slows down, possibly shifting to encephalographic alpha waves associated with rest and relaxation (Iaccino 1993: 119, 131). Interhemispheric activity can thus occur through the dominance or metacontrol of one hemisphere supplemented by the other. In the case of linguistic activity, the dominance of the LH is confirmed by observations of right ear auditory advantage. These observations regarding verbal processing activity point to three complementary phenomena: the greater efficiency of contralateral nerve pathways; the suppression of auditory information transmitted through left-side ipsilateral connections; and the transfer of right-side ipsilateral information to the LH via the corpus callosum.

Our understanding of brain lateralization, however, becomes all the more complex when we consider the unevenness of hemispheric specialization. When asymmetries are found using tachistoscopic tasks and other procedures, left-brain functions tend to be more pronounced relative to right-brain advantages.

This uneven specialization phenomenon comes out quite clearly in studies of "hemispheric attention" behaviour, to which we now turn.

Hemispheric superiority hinges not only on the actual task to be performed but also on contextual conditions and anticipations. Expectations regarding an activity and stimuli perceived immediately before a given task is performed may activate one of the two hemispheres. This brain pre-activity may involve an attentional disposition (cortical, sensorial, physical) to receive and process information predominantly on one side and in the corresponding mode. Studies suggest that hemispheric attentional biases vary considerably from one individual or population to another (e.g., the right-handed vs. the left-handed). Observed differences may reflect variations in cognitive styles, hence preferred information-processing strategies that may be adopted regardless of the task at hand (Iaccino 1993: 121–4; Hugdahl 1995: 151). Individual variations in attentional dispositions are particularly important in this regard. As Bruder (1995: 663) points out, although dichotic and visual half-field tests "typically yield a right ear/field advantage for verbal tasks and a left ear/field advantage for nonverbal tasks, considerable individual differences are found in the magnitude and direction of perceptual asymmetry." Since about 25 per cent of normal right-handed adults show unexpected ear advantages on dichotic listening tests, important variations can be thought to affect how individuals actually use and activate their right and left hemispheres.

Using dichotic and tachistoscopic procedures, Bryden (1986) argues that hemispheric advantages can be heightened through instructions to *focus* on stimulation coming from one side of the body or the other. The left brain, however, shows a greater capacity to concentrate on what it does best. When cued to specific inputs, the LH voluntary-attention effect (attending to the right field) tends to be greater and more stable than its RH counterpart. In other words, when deploying *focused* attention, the analytic-minded hemisphere shows an advantage over the right-holistic mind.

By contrast, RH attentionality is underfocused and therefore less specialized. The RH frontal lobe is good at accomplishing tasks that are complex and demand a high level of general attention, without previous hints announcing the kind of task to be performed. This holds true irrespective of the stimulus material involved, be it verbal or spatial (Iaccino 1993: 127). This observation tallies with the fact that the right brain has greater capacity to attend to both contralateral and ipsilateral sides of the body. But it is also reinforced by the tendency for normal subjects' general attention to be slightly biased towards the left visual field (Heilman 1995). When compared to left-brain impairments, anesthesia and lesions of the RH will there-fore result in reduced levels of arousal, which is the readiness to process incoming stimuli or to increase the overall signal-to-noise ratio. Likewise, RH damages will affect observed levels of vigilance.

The RH plays a greater role in processes of diffuse attention, arousal, and vigilance. Lesions to this hemisphere will therefore result in a greater frequency and severity of problems of con-tralateral neglect (or hemineglect) and extinction. These prob-lems occur when patients fail to report contralesional stimuli in situations of simultaneous bilateral stimulation. (Note that stimuli may be visual, tactile, or auditive but may also originate from dreams.) Injuries to the right inferior parietal lobes are more likely to produce symptoms of neglect; this is where internal sensory mapping attentionality is primarily located (Rosenzweig et al. 1999: 550). Lastly, given that the RH is less focused and spends more time paying attention to the same stimuli (which means a slower rate of habituation), impair-ments to this hemisphere tend to result in greater inattention problems (Heilman 1995: 227).

The analytic mind used to be considered more important to the human species compared to our "minor" thinking pro-cesses, deemed to be instinctive and brutish. If overdeveloped, the "inferior" operations of right-brain thinking could lead to madness – so thought Luys and Delaunay, after Broca. Both cognitive modes are now viewed as essential to complex brain activity. But if so, why this uneven specialization of the two hemispheres? Could it be that the higher level of left-brain functionalization points to the importance of language in the evolution of the human species? Or does the observed phenomenon simply reflect the centrality of analytic thought and writing-reading-arithmetic in western culture, as claimed by Orstein (Iaccino 1993: 114–15)?

Many argue one side or the other of this debate by pitting evolutionary universalism against cultural particularism. But there is an alternative explanation. The unequal specialization of the two hemispheres may have something to do with the uneven interdependence that lies between the two brains. We know that LH activities cannot do without the holistic, visuospatial input of the RH. For instance, a correct left-brain perception of the differences that lie between the sounds *t* and *d*, the letters *A* and *B* and the digits 1 and 2 requires a right-brain recognition of their similarities. Resemblance lies in the presence of two palatal sounds, the first two letters of the western alphabet, and the first two integers of our decimal system, respectively. For "local" distinctions to be made (as between *A* and *B*), the "global" fields that bring conspecific elements together (the western alphabet) must be properly recognized. Note that this field-dependent information need not be consciously attended. Much of the supplementary information provided by the gestalt brain can simply be thrown into the background, allowing details and specific moments in time to receive a greater share of brain attentionality. That is, common-denominator information is of secondary importance compared to the act of discrimination that permits the subject to differentiate between paired sounds, letters, and numbers. Likewise, the task of recognizing field conspecificity requires less consciousness compared to placing signs of language in their proper sequential order (A before B). Given that discrimination and sequencing are particularly important to speech production, the LH is obliged to take the lead in monitoring what is a bilateral speech apparatus in all other respects (see Peters 1995: 202).

The same cannot be said of the RH. The gestalt brain functions differently in that the information it receives from the "analytic mind" may be so critical that the LH cannot be pushed into the background. For instance, an overall facial configuration or object can be identified by the RH only if the subject pays considerable LH attention to the diacritic features of the visual material processed by the brain. Take away Hitler's unique moustache, and most people might take more time to recognize the man's face. Although the two hemispheres tend to accomplish different tasks, some activities are more functionally interdependent than others. Compared to the LH, the holistic hemisphere appears to be more dependent on whole brain activity.

A Childless Father
and a Rose Is a Rose

Neuroscientific studies of the brain represent a breakthrough in western thinking about the mind. Neuropsychology transforms the way we talk about thinking. The mind is no longer a metaphysical entity vaguely lodged in the head, an intellect hovering above the (rest of the) human body. Nor is it a unified soul, as Flourens and other nineteenth-century opponents of phrenology used to claim. The human *esprit* (Fr., mind) is an infinitely complex organism yet a palpable thing, with distinguishable functions that can be broken down into component parts and interrelated processes.

Still, the half-brain literature reviewed above is faced with a riddle. How can the brain represent itself and its component parts through the language of science? That is, how can specialized parts of the brain reflect on whole brain activity, and how can the whole brain reflect on specialized parts of everyone's mind? The riddle is not a convoluted exercise in recursivity – asking questions about ways to know what knowledge is all about. Talking about the words we use to "speak of language" is as important as thinking about the way we "think of thinking." Empirical analyses of hemispheric functions are essential to our understanding of the natural grounding of Descartes's cogito. All the same, the notion that we have direct access to an observational language that can describe these "mental" processes without imposing a particular perspective on reality goes against the little we know about how the brain actually works!

RIGHT (visual)	LEFT (auditive)
Gestalt (whole)	Logic (parts)
Similarities	Differences
Images, meaning	Numbers, letters
Emotion, intuition	Reasoning, analysis
Rhythm, flow	Sequentiality
Humour, mood	Literal focus
Far-sightedness	Details, technique

Characterizing the cognitive processes of each hemisphere is no easy task since it requires prior knowledge of the basic functions of brain activity. The problem is that the knowledge we already have is rather limited and tends to be marred by pre-established concepts derived from particular paradigms. As Churchland (1986: 148) remarks, "even determining what the general categories of higher functions are is a deeply empirical-theoretical task, and it is becoming increasingly evident that in a literal sense we do not yet understand *what* 'higher' capacities the brain has, or whether conventional categories come even closer to carving Nature at her proverbial joints." The author adds:

if the psychological (functional) taxonomy is ill defined, then the search for neural substrates for those functions will be correspondingly ill defined ... The treacherous difficulty here is that we cannot be sure when we are asking the right questions. We do not know whether such categories as "emotion," "declarative memory," "procedural memory," "learning," and "consciousness" pick out a unified, single, *natural* kind, or whether these categories herd together quite motley collections of disparate phenomena – whether searching for the neural substrate for "memory" is like looking for the "principle" that unites jewels, such as amethysts, diamonds, amber, and pearls.

Jewels do not form a *natural kind*, in the sense that there are natural laws about their properties and behavior. They are *accidental kinds*, unified not by their nature but by social convention. It may be that commonsense theory (folk psychology) is so misconceived, and its taxonomy so askew, that even the formulation of our questions thwarts our inquiry (152).

The problem is that categories used to portray the two cognitive modes are often presented as empirically grounded terms that reflect observable differences and that are readily intelligible and relatively simple. These include dyads such as the analytic and the synthetic, the rational and the emotional, the verbal-auditive and the visual-spatial, the diachronic (temporal) and the synchronic (atemporal), the motive and the emotive. The problem with these received binarisms is threefold.

First, dyadic terms applied to cognitive differences between the two brains are sometimes too comprehensive, using complex bihemispheric activities to characterize functions deemed to be specific to one hemisphere only. Terms are so encompassing that they tend to gloss over the bihemispheric implications of functions attributed to each side of the brain.

Second, there are instances where hemispheric labels widely accepted in neuropsychology may not be encompassing enough. This is the case when hemispheric attributes are simply listed, without more general terms to capture the common denominators of each series. The same problem emerges when a function (e.g., the analytic) is used to define the entire hemisphere but without a theory that shows how other same-hemisphere functions (e.g., sequentiality) follow from the defining attribution.

Last but not least, the literature is so "scientifically oriented" that it may be suspected of understanding whole brain activity with the use of cognitive tools and models borrowed from one hemisphere only. The LH "analytic" mind usually does the job, with its propensity towards dualities and contrast-generalizations. Paradoxically, this analytic bias is not without its own right-brain gestalt-perspective on what brain activity is all about. As we shall see, the preferred perspective tends to be that of cognitivism, which is but one possible synthesis applied to the brain lateralization phenomenon.

These three problems reinforce Churchland's warning concerning the use of terms and categories derived from conventional psychological wisdom. But they also reflect a deeper problem: a tendency to answer questions about brain lateralization with the use of *categories that are taken for granted* and insufficiently problematized, never to be treated as complex neuropsychological functions in their own right. In reality, concepts of analytic rationality, spatiality, attentionality, emotionality, and temporality are no less in need of grounding than the hemispheric divide. More must be known about what recognizable processes these functions entail before they can be used as legitimate categories applicable to brain lateralization studies. Without this grounding, studies of brain lateralization run the risk of reproducing an older divide: the language of biology to denote brain parts and that of cognitive psychology to describe their functions. In lieu of reuniting brain and mind, neuropsychology may end up offering mere correlations between neurology and psychology. Bringing the two disciplines into a single field may promise more than what it actually delivers.

THE ANALYTIC AND THE SYNTHETIC

Of all labels used to characterize lateral brain functions, concepts such as the analytic and the synthetic are among the most helpful in suggesting differential emphases on the whole or the parts. The terms point to hemispheric attentions to either the overall configuration or the precise details of a stimulus situation. These terms, however, can hardly subsume other discriminating factors such as the auditive, temporal, rational, visual, spatial, or emotive. What is more, the evocations of things analytic or synthetic are so far reaching and so closely attached to particular epistemologies that they may not be the most appropriate in capturing the universals of brain activity.

The word *analysis* denotes a cognitive process whereby the whole is broken down into various parts or its simplest elements. Things are thus "loosened up" (Gr. *ana*, up, back, and *lysis*, a

loosing) in ways that reveal their internal composition. By contrast, the word *synthesis* means a "putting together" (Gr. *syn*,
together, and *tithenai*, to place). In positivistic philosophy, however, these terms evoke an older distinction that was to have a
considerable impact on the development of modern science. We
know that Kant played a key role in developing this distinction.
He premised his philosophy of knowledge on the notion that
what must be in the logical sense differs from *what is* in the
empirical sense. While an analytic judgment employs a predicate
that is contained in the subject ("a square has four equal recti-
linear sides"), a synthetic judgment offers a predicate that adds
something to the subject, something that cannot be known through
logical reasoning alone ("this building has a square shape").

About a century ago, G.E. Moore, one of the founders of
analytic philosophy, expounded his own "commonsense" perspective on the analytic-synthetic distinction, insisting that a
grounded approach to knowledge and language be substituted
for all forms of metaphysical speculation. Although for different
reasons, Russell insisted as well on the necessity to explore and
develop the inner logic and forms of propositions, towards the
production of a mathematical language purified from theology
and metaphysics. The early Wittgenstein converted Russell's
quest for a new mathematics into a reflection on the structure
of logic embedded in both language and reality, hence meaningful statements that are logical and factual all at once. By the
1930s and 1940s, however, logical positivists of the Vienna
Circle (Schlick, Carnap, Godel) claimed that in order to make
sense, analytic sentences should be verified or refuted with synthetic observations of reality, using experience and the senses
to test our knowledge about the world. In *Language, Truth,
and Logic* (1936), Ayer drives a similar argument home. Philosophy must be first and foremost an exercise in the logic of
language, searching for analytic propositions that are both true
by convention (as with mathematical tautologies) and empirically meaningful. Logical propositions are worth pursuing if
they make a contribution to science by means of synthetic
statements that can be verified and established by experience.

Some concrete examples are in order. "My father is childless" is illogical and therefore analytically false. There is no need to test the statement against experience to spot the error. "A rose is a rose" is analytically true but synthetically meaningless and uninformative. When transposed to the field of neuropsychology, the "childless father" phrase could be said to offend our LH concern for breaking down things that should logically be kept apart; in this instance, fatherhood and childlessness. Conversely, "a rose is a rose" brings together things that are so "identical" as to be in no need of being reunited through RH activity. We might say that each hemisphere decides whether or not the proposition is an insult to its synthetic or analytic intelligence. The brain lateralization phenomenon would thus appear to confirm positivistic views of knowledge.

But things are not that simple. When closely examined, the digital approach to products of the brain – either analytic or synthetic, either meaningful or meaningless, either true or false – does little justice to the subtle interconnections of cognitive activity.

Although trivial, the childless-father and a-rose-is-a-rose examples point to a flaw in the analytic-synthetic literature: its overemphasis on rules of lateral differentiation as opposed to the intricacies of whole brain activity. Each sentence is problematical not because of its rejection by one hemisphere or the other. Hemispheric objections point rather to problems of *interhemispheric noise* – dissonance between responses obtained from the two sides of the brain. To say that my father is childless is to do three things simultaneously:

1 select a particular semantic field, i.e., kinship terms;
2 signify two determinate positions within that field (fatherhood, childlessness); and then
3 establish a relationship of identity between the two conspecific terms.

The left brain is offended by a failure to recognize the incompatibility between "fatherhood" and "childlessness." But the right brain is no less active. It must recognize the common field (kinship) posited by this sentence for the "analytic error" to be spotted in the first place. Thanks to RH processing, a "childless father" becomes a logical contradiction, as opposed to something purely meaningless (e.g., a "rectangular father").

A similar bihemispheric dialogue feeds into the assessment of synthetic meaning (be it analytically true or false). The tautologous fault undermining the statement of "a rose is a rose" points indeed to a bihemispheric judgment. The assessment consists in a right brain refusing to "pull things together" due to a left brain noticing an impossibility to distinguish. At best the RH can recognize "a rose" when it sees a rose, but this can hardly be interpreted as a *fully fledged synthetic proposition* containing empirically meaningful information. An LH recognition of the different component parts organized into a synthesis is essential for the act of synthesis to occur. As we shall see later, cognitive efforts to "pull together" elements of reality are profoundly dependent on our capacity to "break down" everything we wish to assemble.

By contrast, a sentence that is both analytically acceptable and synthetically informative, such as "this rose was given to me by my son," puts both sides of the brain to work without creating interhemispheric noise. Speakers and listeners can recreate the overall scene integrating elements taken from learnt codes that are distinguishable (plant categories differ from human categories) and that generate internal distinctions, such as between father and son, a rose and other kinds of flowers, the act of giving and the act of receiving.

Admittedly, when describing lateral brain differences, neuropsychologists do not commit themselves to the tenets of logical positivism. Remnants of positivism are nonetheless reintroduced through back-door notions such as the abstract and the concrete, terms that are usually assigned to the analytic and the synthetic hemispheres respectively (Iaccino 1993: 64). The right brain is often said to have a predilection for words that are high-frequency and concrete, terms that are relatively "simple" and "familiar." Although commonly embraced, the argument is not without problems. For one thing, words such as "abstract" and "concrete" are relatively abstract. This is so true that translating these concepts into non Indo-European languages represents a difficult task. More importantly, the term "abstract" can easily be assimilated to the simple instead of the complex. The term expresses the quality of something that has been "drawn or separated from" something else, especially from mental representations of particular instances and material objects. Expressions such as "being abstracted by thoughts of the morrow" or "writing an abstract" imply acts of separation; they drag something away from something else, be it one's immediate attention or the essential thoughts of a book. This means that the more global and united we perceive things to be, the more concrete they are. By contrast, the more local and separate our perception is, the more abstract it becomes. Far from signifying things that are complex, words and propositions deemed to be abstract must avoid the complexity of full objects, contexts, and speech processes requiring RH processing capabilities. If this is true, leftover concepts of positivistic inspiration pitting the simple against the complex and the concrete against the abstract are of little service in making sense of the brain lateralization phenomenon.

THE RATIONAL AND THE EMOTIONAL

In keeping with the objectivity and emotion-free principles of positivism, the analytic/synthetic paradigm suggests a purely cognitive approach to lateral functions of the brain. Hemispheric labels will thus work provided we "abstract" intellectual functions from other aspects of our psyche. I hasten to add that this problem could always be remedied by *treating emotionality as a cognitive mode* in its own right. Emotionality is a processing activity sensitive to tone, mood, and affect, a style of knowing that tallies with the RH predilection for concrete images and thoughts.

This notion of "emotive intelligence" is a definite improvement on older notions of "brainless emotionality." Theories of cognitive emotionality will help put a damper on religious-scientific claims according to which the growth of left-brain language and analytic thought capabilities in humans allows them to transcend all other living species and communicate with the Creator via the Verb and his Word. The notion that our left brain is the repository of Logos in humans created in the image of their Creator is an oversimplification of neuropsychology, to say the least (Ashbrook 1988). Neuropsychology has advanced our understanding of the multiple aspects of intellectual and linguistic activity, which include complex right-brain processes.

Despite newly gained concessions to "emotive thinking," neurocognitive studies are still inclined to give the worn-out affect/intellect clichés a new hemispheric credibility. Models that wire the right brain to emotionality and the left to rationality can be suspected of being culturally biased. Little anthropological imagination is needed to see in this affect/intellect binarism a cultural and philosophical distinction that should not be granted a universal biological standing.

Lateralization models that divide the rational from the emotive generate several other major difficulties. Firstly, studies of emotionality should account for the different operations involved in the decoding and the encoding of affect. As Davidson (1995: 364) puts it, care must be taken in "differentiating among different components of emotional functioning, most importantly between the perception of emotion and the expression of emotion." What is even more critical is that we avoid confusing the cognitive processing of emotive input and output with the actual experience of emotionality. Though interrelated, encoding and decoding emotive information is not the same as experiencing an actual feeling and related effects of physiological arousal. There tends to be considerable confusion between the two. This leads some students of neuroscience concerned mostly with cognitive activity to characterize the RH *cognitive* mode as emotional rather than rational. This is a relatively old idea that does little justice to the role of subcortical inputs in emotional experience and the interaction between neocortical and subcortical systems in emotional activity proper.

Secondly, RH connections between emotionality and synthetic thinking are by no means self-evident. Actually, emotionality is at odds with the positivistic precept of synthetic perceptual objectivity, a contradiction that points to the arbitrary and list-like labelling of hemispheric activities. This chaotic shopping-list approach to brain lateralization is sometimes turned into a theoretical virtue. "There is no such thing as *the* laterality function that can be assessed with whatever laterality task or test. Each hemisphere subserves multiple functions that need not correlate with one another," claims Hugdahl (1995: 123). Sergent makes the same point when she claims that "it is now clear that the search for a single, bipolar principle that would encompass the functional properties of the two hemispheres would be futile" (1995: 178). Monolithic oversimplifications of cerebral functions should certainly be avoided. All the same, neuropsychologists should not insist on reducing the brain lateralization phenomenon to an eclectic sum of empirical observations and discrete operations assigned to each hemisphere.

Thirdly, empirical studies suggest that emotionality is not the property of one hemisphere alone. Studies of hemispheric paralysis involving sodium amytal injections have reported extreme emotional reactions for paralyses on both sides of the brain: disphoria in the case of left-sided injections (arresting the so-called linear-rational brain), and indifference or euphoria in the case of right-sided injections (arresting the so-called holistic-emotive brain). Instead of leaving all emotions intact, damage to the left frontal lobe may cause depressive symptomatology. Pathological crying is known to be associated with LH injuries, and pathological laughing with injuries on the right side (Iaccino 1993: 61). Facial expression tests suggest that the left side of the face (RH) displays stronger feelings. The right side (LH), however, is not without emotions. When subjects are asked to describe the feelings produced by lifting each corner of their mouths, asymmetrical states are commonly reported, "with more negative feelings of sadness and depression being correlated to the left-sided (right-hemispheric) contractions and more positive feelings of happiness and general contentment being associated with right-sided (left-hemispheric) contractions" (ibid.: 134–5).

These results indicate that each hemisphere has emotional dispositions of its own. This may be due to the actual nature of cognitive activities controlled by each brain. When working alone, the right brain may be trapped into a given mood and context. It may have no sense of how to engage in sequential activities that will allow the subject to attain particular end-goals, doing it one step at a time and moving through all related states. Feelings of immobility, powerlessness, and sadness may ensue. By contrast, when disconnected from the RH, the left brain may become obsessed with moving forward from one action to another. This may be done at the expense of keeping track of the overall context and larger goals, background information that gives meaning to motions in time. The consequences of obsessive left-brain activity may consist in a reduced sense of direction in space and time and the resulting experience of indifference, confusion, nervousness, or anxiety.

But the idea that each cognitive mode is associated with the expression of specific affects tells us little about the biology and neurology of emotionality proper. This brings us to the final point. Whatever emotional profile can be assigned to each hemisphere, cognitive theories of brain lateralization should not isolate themselves from studies of other brain systems. Cognitive processes mapped along the sagittal plane (right-left) are directly conditioned by the axial chemistry (cortical-subcortical) of affect and judgment and by the coronal anatomy (anterior-posterior) of remembering and planning. In order to be fully understood, hemispheric activities should be studied against the background of what we know about the neuropsychology of feeling and the passing of time, topics to be discussed at length in *The 3-D Mind* 2 and 3.

THE AUDITIVE-DIACHRONIC-TEMPORAL AND THE VISUAL-SYNCHRONIC-SPATIAL

We now turn to the contrast between the left-brain predilection for relations of sequentiality and the right-brain preference for relations of simultaneity. The opposition is often tied to yet another dichotomy: the verbal-auditive and the visual-spatial, one system functioning diachronically (going through one step after another) and the other synchronically (with an emphasis on simultaneous relations in space). These distinctions are empirically appealing. Nonetheless, it's important to remember that verbal-auditory and visual-spatial activities are complex. Therefore they are bound to receive the combined input of both hemispheres. They also vary considerably, which means that particular verbal and visual tasks may differ in the specialized hemispheric abilities they actually tap and combine. Take verbal activity, for instance. As studies of surface dyslexia show, language read or spoken adds up to more than left-brain words and grammar uttered, written, or comprehended without the help of right-brain semantics, tonal expression, and context-information processing (Peters 1995: 198). Similarly, right-brain visualizations add up to little when deprived of the finer sequential motions and discriminating functions of the LH. As Hellige (1995) argues, each hemisphere processes visual information differently. The LH specializes in local aspects and categorical relations in space (above/under, off/on). It is also well equipped to process high frequencies, i.e., sharper images consisting of smaller, non-overlapping visual fields. By contrast, the right brain is biased towards global aspects, coordinate relations in space (e.g., relative distance), and low visuospatial frequencies.

The same subtle hemispheric differences have been observed in studies of auditory processing and motor performance. Compared to the right ear and hand, the left ear and hand (RH processing) are better at detecting low-frequency sounds and performing broader movements, respectively. Using both ears concurrently is like using both hands at the same time: each hemisphere complements the other by making different temporal and attentional demands on the whole brain. Asymmetrical attention is involved here in that more focused attention is usually granted to the right side of the body (LH), at least among right-handers; "Attention is asymmetrically distributed in right-handers, favoring the right hand when both hands compete for attention" (Peters 1995: 201). But the implication here is not that the LH is working while the RH is at rest. Rather "it is argued that not only is attention asymmetrically distributed to the two hands but that this is the essential prerequisite for skilled bimanual activity" (ibid.; see also Liotti and Tucker 1995: 392).

There is another problem with the temporal-auditive/spatial-visual contrast: it does not necessarily fit in with or follow from previous distinctions such as the analytic and the synthetic. Take the connection between temporality and analytic thinking, both of which are typically assigned to the LH. The connection is by no means a necessary one. The brain can be kept analytically busy without engaging in measurements of time. For instance, it can tackle an exercise of logical classification without using rules of temporal or serial framing. Notwithstanding speculations about the evolution of canine species, the analytic distinction between *canis canis* (dog) and *canis lupus* (wolf) is part of a zoological code that requires no reference to sequentiality.

In any case, the time factor is not an uncompounded aspect of reality that can be processed by one hemisphere alone, the left. The RH is not insensitive to the unfolding of time: quite the contrary. Given its synthetic inclination, the right brain is well attuned to the production and recognition of notes of continuity over time, notes that generate a tone or a mood. This is an important aspect of temporality that should not be confused with mere sequentiality. The apprehension of tone and mood allows the gestalt brain to play a leading role in processing regularities over time, the kind that sound patterns but also attitudes and states of mind are made of. This patterning and plotting of time is what the brain does when converting moments in sequence into stories and narratives, producing time-contextual linkages between memories, immediate perceptions, and expectations of things to come. Without the RH, there is no thread in time.

Interestingly, Iaccino (1993: 42) reports that greater activity in the RH "has been recorded in Hopis when they listened to stories in their native language." The observation confirms one of two things. It may suggest "that this particular culture is more right modal," as Iaccino would have it. Or it may indicate that the right brain is particularly active when subjects are hearing a good story – grasping a plot constructed through narrative time. The latter hypothesis is reinforced by observations of right-lesioned patients who are at pains to tell or summarize a brief story (Churchland 1986: 188). In keeping with this reasoning, studies of attentionality show that when subjects are asked to get ready for an undefined stimulus situation (involving an unknown task that may appeal to one hemisphere or the other), the RH shows a greater capacity to sustain the attention.

The RH thus responds to the time factor in its own way. It has an inherent disposition to follow the narrative thread of language and also to "wait and see" for things that may eventually come as a surprise (or not). Again, these observations imply that there is more to time than mere sequentiality. As *The 3-D Mind 3* argues at some length, this is an important qualification that applies to all tasks involving the time factor and the complex operations of memory and planning.

SPATIALIZED COGNITIVISM

Conventional categories applied to differences between the right and left hemispheres are problematical. To some extent the difficulty lies in the scientific pursuit of cognitive typologies. However refined they may be, classificatory exercises are faced with serious limitations. When seeking explanation through contrast-generalization, neuropsychology ends up short-changing the hemispheric lateralization phenomenon. It is as if the discipline chose a left-brain, "analytic" approach to its subject matter rather than a whole-brain comprehension of cerebral rightness and leftness. A propensity to break things down into their component parts and attributes prevails, to the detriment of a synthetic "pulling together" of the manifold functions governing each hemisphere and full brain activity. Neuropsychology thus boils down to the "idea that the brain is organized into distinct areas of relative functional autonomy and specialization is a basic principle of cognitive neuroscience" (Sergent 1995: 157). This means that "to locate the material base for a piece of mind is to claim it for science," with the implication that "to break mind down into its brain-based building blocks is to know it" (Harrington 1995: 4).

This take-to-pieces approach carries the legacy of organology or phrenology, the assessment of mental faculties on the basis of skull measurements propounded by Franz Joseph Gall in the early nineteenth century. Gall's approach was based on assumptions of strict cerebral localization. The mind is located inside the brain, with composite parts that have unequal sizes and that serve distinct mental faculties. The human mind and brain are subject to an overall division of labour organized hierarchically, with the frontal-lobe intellect dominating the rear-lobe animal instincts and affects. Current reformulations of spatialized cognitivism date back to these early scientific views of the mind and related battles of science against theological claims to knowledge of spirit and soul.

Gall thought of speech as having a cerebral organ resembling the heart or liver and working "as a discrete, largely independent, island-like entity. Certainly that model of cortical specialization, as applied to the entire spectrum of psychological functions, ran afoul of the evidence that the whole brain is involved in varying degrees in intelligent functions and in memory" (Churchland 1986: 161).

Studies of brain injuries and their impact on cognitive activities and human behaviour have been important tools in developing the view that each cognitive function has a brain centre of its own. As Churchland argues, these studies are not without their limitations. "For one thing, the area A might be *necessary* for the function Y, without being both necessary *and* sufficient as the description 'center' implies. Moreover, lesions in area A might result in interference with other brain areas that are critical for Y, without A itself being either necessary or sufficient for Y. It is known that acute lesions may disturb functions elsewhere in the brain ... and a behavioral deficit may be the result of such secondary, nonspecific causes (also called 'diaschisis'). Finally, there might be no 'center' for Y at all" (164).

Lesion data can serve to identify the function of an area provided that a lesion be the only one to consistently produce a particular deficit. The deficit in question must be measured appropriately and objectively and with intervening variables (age, etiology, etc.) being controlled. Otherwise all other things cannot be deemed to be equal. Without data of this sort, the notion that A is the centre for Y tends to be abandoned in favour of "A has elements underlying the function Y," or "A is involved with Y" (Churchland 1986: 165). In short, great caution is required to establish brain area specialization and also the exact language to capture discrete brain functions.

As already suggested, the ways in which science carves out the brain often reinforce dualities pivotal to western history and philosophy. One localizable "mind-set" is spread around the world via the apparently neutral language of neuroscience. Contrasts between holistic intuition and sequential-analytic logic are overgeneralized and taken out of the mindset that gives them meaning. It's a short step from this approach to empirical studies suggesting correlations between hemisphericity and personality structure, occupation, gender, and culture. Part of this literature claims that men, lawyers, and western cultures are more left-minded, hence preoccupied with time, logical-analytic reasoning, arithmetic, verbalization, and phonocentric literacy. By contrast, women and artists are more right-minded. So are native and eastern societies, people who place value on meditation, visualization, experiential learning, altered states of consciousness, and holistic thinking. These comparative analyses (Iaccino 1993: 40–1, 46–7, 53) are laudably committed to the understanding and appreciation of diversity in cognitive processes and human behaviour. Studies that use the brain lateralization phenomenon to make sense of differences between genders, populations, and cultures should nonetheless be careful not to elevate western binarisms to the rank of descriptive universals founded in biology. Dichotomies such as the linear versus the holistic do not provide solid foundations for comparative analyses in social psychology or cultural anthropology. Neuropsychology should be particularly wary of the dangers of voguish "dichotomania," a cerebral manichaeism that often pits LH "logomania" against romantic notions of right-brain "metaphoria."

It may be that the riddle of scientific brains reflecting and talking about everyone's whole brain is insurmountable. Neuropsychology is perhaps bound to generate a left-brain discourse on cerebral hemisphericity. Given its analytic methods, science may be in no position to grasp the interconnections that coordinate the two hemispheres in complex and variable ways. But science has tools to be critical of everything, including itself. The notion that particular tasks can be assigned to one hemisphere or the other can be challenged on scientific grounds. As Hellige (1995: 100) suggests, cognitive science should adopt a componential approach, a perspective based on models where activities are decomposed into specific components that can contribute to a wide range of tasks. The implication is that "both hemispheres are normally involved in one way or another in almost everything we do, even though their contributions may differ." The same argument is made by Sergent:

Psychological and cognitive functions are no longer viewed as made of unitary processes (e.g., reading, writing, object recognition) but rather as being composed of several subprocesses (e.g., feature analysis, structural encoding, activation of biographic memories) organized in specific ways (e.g., in parallel or in succession, independently or interactively), and the cognitive architecture of mental functions is best characterized by a compartmented organization of interactive components. It is therefore through a decomposition of a given function into its component operations, thus providing a theoretical framework specifying the nature, the goals, the logical order, and the interactive relations of the processing steps to be performed for the realization of the function under study, that a better specification of the functional organization of the cerebral cortex can be achieved. The understanding of brain-behavior relationships can then be conceived of as an enterprise that aims at mapping a fractionated set of interrelated mental operations underlying cognitive functions onto their corresponding interconnected cerebral structures (1995: 157).

Given this rule of "cerebral teamwork," a fully developed modelling of the brain requires that all aspects of brain inter-activity be explored. Incidentally, this includes activities that go beyond differences mapped along the right-left sagittal plane. Harrington (1995: 22) points out that "studies on the functional significance of the right-left lateral axis tend more often to be qualified along frontal-caudal and cortical-subcortical axes." As we shall see in *The 3-D Mind* 2 and 3, longitudinal and vertical axes have a direct bearing on our understanding of hemispheric asymmetry and whole brain activity.

The idea that whole brain activity is essential to specialized brain processes is not new, as Churchland explains. It dates back to evolutionary theories of the 1860s. The British neurologist John H. Jackson used concepts borrowed from Herbert Spencer to propose

an integrated set of systems organized in a hierarchy, with sensori-motor representation featured at every level but with increasing complexity and sophistication. Accordingly, his way of reconciling the discrepancies between the "discrete organs" hypothesis and the "holistic" hypothesis was first to replace the exact margins espoused by organ theory with imprecise boundaries and then to argue for multiple representation in various places at various levels of the hierarchies. This implied a division of labor in the nervous system, but a division made many times over, a division that was fuzzy, overlapping, partially redundant, and increasingly specialized; and moreover, a division of labor that had the potential for reorganization in the event of damage. On Jackson's hypothesis, with the destruction of high-level structures the more complicated versions of behavior would also be impaired, but so long as the lower-level structures were intact, simpler "low-level" versions would remain (162).

But whether old or new, warnings concerning science's partiality to left-brain thinking and related hemispheric dualisms should not be overstated. In point of fact neuropsychology does pay considerable attention to brain functions that go beyond hemispheric dualities. Neuroscience is a complex field of research and argumentation well equipped to withstand the most vigorous attacks. Even if it were found to be flawed, neuropsychology should still be recognized for what it is: a product of language, an elaborate expression of whole brain activity. However analytically inclined it may be, neuroscientific discourse and research on cognitive processes is bound to be a two-hemispheric production in its own right. Half-brain talk usually places emphasis on cognitive differences, but it has to deploy considerable linguistic and cognitive activity if it is to lay out its own paradigm and corresponding perspective on human thinking. This cannot be done without a right-brain reconnaissance of the common terrain within which differences are to be addressed by the left brain, so to speak. Neuropsychology must work within an identifiable terrain establishing common denominators that underlie modes and functions deemed to differ in all other respects. In short, theorists cannot advance "analytic" (LH) generalizations regarding hemispheric differences without a gestalt-synthesis or RH bias of their own.

This brings us to a central question: what is the common denominator underlying the component parts of the brain as depicted in the scientific lateralization literature? Is there an overall gestalt-like perspective hiding beneath emphases on brain asymmetry? What is the thread that runs through all those fine weavings of half-brain studies? As already noted, the answer lies partly in the concept of localized function, a frame of reference that puts the emphasis on where cognitive functions are located in the brain as opposed to how they interconnect (Temple 1993: 54). But the answer lies in the premises of cognitivism as well. The two hemispheric profiles have in common that they are *knowing machines* essentially dedicated to information-processing activities. Paradoxically, this integrated perspective embedded in half-brain talk purports to be comprehensive and *is* holistic in its own right.

In *spatialized cognitivism* lies the current synthetic terrain for applying dual analytic thinking to the brain lateralization phenomenon. Readers might object to granting a synthetic, holistic status to cognitivism. After all, the theory precludes other theoretical options. But could it not be that all synthetic operations, including theoretical generalizations, thrive on acts of discrimination – choosing one perspective over another? Could it be that holism to one school is particularism to another? Holistic thought may be only a higher-level analytic discrimination between a synthesis that capture's one attention and another to be ignored. If so, how does cognitivism distinguish itself from contending views? In the sequels to this book, I argue that the answer to this question is to be found in studies of brain dimensions other than the sagittal (RH-LH). Until then, however, we shall ignore studies that go beyond cognitivism, a perspective that emphasizes a brain united and divided along purely cognitive lives (to the exclusion of other dimensions such as emotion and narration).

Meetings of Synkretismos and Diakritikos

Neuropsychology can never transcend its object of study. Half-brain talk is a product of brain activity couched in one language, a discourse subject to cultural and theoretical parochialism of its own. When disassembling the brain, we should therefore ask ourselves "what ingrained cultural values and inherited intellectual assumptions will be discovered to have shaped our own readings of the data" (Harrington 1995: 22). We should also question neuroscience's (LH) binarisms and related (RH) perspective on lateralization, an overall view known as "spatialized cognitivism." Otherwise neuropsychology can misguide us into confusing one particular brain model with the "universal mind."

Does this mean that neuropsychology is a purely arbitrary take on the mind? Should we conclude, as Sir Charles Scott Sherrington once did, that words to adequately represent the impact of different parts of the brain on human behaviour will never be within our reach (cf. ibid.: 5)? Certainly the evidence used for cognitive hemispheric specialization could be more robust than what we now have. But the question is not merely how robust the empirical observations are, a valid question in its own right. A more pressing issue concerns the language we deploy to construct and make sense of the evidence.

As it now stands, neuropsychological discourse on brain lateralization is exceedingly typological. Concepts currently prevailing in the literature tend to privilege an approach that is "logically eccentric" and highly "logocentred" at the same time; that is, students of the brain sort our mental hardware into component parts, functions and categories *orbiting around a centre* called logic or cognition. The end result is a particular "frame of mind," a mindset that emphasizes the intellect as opposed to the affect, thinking as opposed to feeling, discreteness as opposed to fuzziness.

Is there a language to overcome these barriers to a better understanding of the brain? Two choices should be considered here. One is to opt for a technical language, recognizing that new words are needed to compensate for our lack of familiarity with the unknown. Technical jargon might deter us from embedding premises of our culture in the human brain. Another option is to develop an economy of words, terms so simple that they go to the heart of language and thought. While some technical and abstract mumbo jumbo may be unavoidable, a lot may be said about "simple" words that do not carry elaborate descriptive, conceptual, or cultural implications.

"Simples" present two important advantages. First, they may be used to capture the common denominators of things otherwise different. Second, if used flexibly, they may be assigned multiple significations that vary according to context and circumstance. Simple distinctions that are malleable and responsive to variations in context may be better suited to studies of the brain compared to terms that are highly technical, abstract, or cultural. They lend themselves to subtle appropriations and combinations that preclude dualistic mappings of the brain.

But "simples" can also yield simplistic models of the brain, especially if derived from pre-established cultural conventions. Popular depictions of the LH as auditive-analytic and the right as visuospatial-holistic may be a case in point. This half-brain literature, however, does not illustrate the weaknesses of "simples" as defined above. It points rather to an inflexible mapping of differences between sound and sight and between whole and part, a right/left modelling approach that does not permit variable combinations of bipolar terms.

By way of example, the LH is often said to specialize in the processing of bits and pieces of sound. The left cognitive mode takes care of sound and part, as opposed to sight and whole.

We have seen, however, that the RH is good at handling context-sensitive, tonal sound structures. The right brain is equipped to bring sound and whole together. Other instances of combinatory deviations from hemispheric attributions have already been provided. They include interventions of the RH in the processing of time and language and the LH in the processing of affect and visual space. These examples all point in the same direction: flexible ways in which the left and the right hemispheres deal with sound and sight, part and whole, time and space, logic and emotion, all depending on the actual task at hand.

Tasks should not be confused with functions. The former are composite and complex, the latter are simple and combinative. Rather than emphasizing the malleable combination of functions in tasks, models of the brain often fall back on two-column representations of hemispheric specializations. The idea that hemispheric distinctions can be aligned in two-column contrast-imageries is attractive in some respects. For instance, arguments that point to LH affinities between sound, time, and part are plausible. *Verbal activity* thus requires a *serial or sequential* ordering of sounds and words that must be attended one after the other, with a focus on the *component parts* of linguistic communication. Models that point to RH affinities between sight, space, and whole make a lot of sense as well. Visual perceptions of spatial arrangements require a synchronic processing of configurational distances and relations. All in all, right is to left what sight (visual) is to sound (auditive), what space (gestalt) is to time (sequential) and what whole is to part. This correlation of multiple oppositions, however, is misleading in that it fails to distinguish between elementary functions and tasks that require coordination of composite functions. Activities such as speaking, reading, seeing, recognizing faces, or listening to music are far too complex to be attributed to a single hemisphere.

Hemispheric characterizations should be based on "flexible simples." Two questions come immediately to mind, though: what terms should we use to make sense of these, and how many "simples" should there be? Should it be several per hemisphere, or should there be one catch-all word for each brain? Should we rewrite columns of hemispheric attributions using terms that are "simpler," or should we prefer instead an elementary binarism that expresses the common denominators of all those behavioural advantages observed in each hemisphere? As already noted, many neuropsychologists have chosen the multiple-attribution strategy. Hugdahl and Sergent thus claim that there is no overarching bipolar principle to account for the multiple functions of each hemisphere. There is no bipolar terminology that may be "simple" enough to capture commonalties and variations within each hemisphere.

If so, what do cognitive advantages manifested by each hemisphere have in common? Better said, what are the similarities between differences in hemispheric advantages? Lévi-Strauss's answer to these questions lies in the order of similarities and differences. But to use a language less dependent on the legacy of structural linguistics and semiotics, we might say that hemispheric functions point to operations of "syncretic" and "diacritic" processing, two "simple" processes that combine in complex ways to produce multiple bihemispheric tasks.

In what sense do these terms capture the hemispheric later-alization phenomenon? Consider the connection between LH advantages and diacritic processing, from the Greek word *diakritikos*, to separate, to divide, to distinguish. Briefly, the ability of the LH to perceive and produce concrete differences in speech sound and to organize discrete phonemes and morphemes serially, putting them into proper phonetic and grammatical order, is at the root of all linguistic activity. The LH shows a definite advantage in processing these *auditory distinctions in space and time*. This tallies with the left brain focus on arithmetic and writing – hence numbers, letters, and words forming systems of encoded differences arranged in meaningful succession, through syntagmatic rules. Thanks to these rules, we can distinguish *pit* from *tip*, and 12 from 21. Numerical, verbal, and inscriptive specifications of the left brain are also in keeping with the left-analytic focus on visuospatial details. The LH breaks things down into small discernible parts and pays "focused attention" to the salient features and sequential ordering of perceived objects. Finally, this ability to differentiate and discern "local" elements in space and time coincides with a left-brain control over precise motor actions performed in sequence. The activities listed here require bihemispheric input, yet they all manifest a preponderance of left-brain diacritic processing, be it visual or auditory.

By contrast, the RH predilection for visual configurations and relations of simultaneity in space and time points to what might be called "syncretic" processing, from the Greek word *synkretismos*, the union of two parties. To syncretize is to unite, blend, fuse, reconcile, or harmonize. The gestalt brain acts syncretically when generating global perceptions of simple forms and geometric figures (Brown and Kosslyn 1995: 79). Syncretic processing is crucial to the RH advantage in assembling things that go together (e.g., pictures of snow and a shovel) and also parts with whole (e.g., the moustache to match Hitler's face). The capacity to unite allows us to identify a familiar object or person, attaching names and associations of all sorts to precise objects and people. It makes it possible to connect an overall mood to an overall facial expression. Syncretism also generates metaphors and all near-identity relationships, the kind that connect a symbol to what it resembles or stands for (the cross for Christ or Christianity). The perception of unity permits us to recognize the tonal aspects or sustained frequencies of a speech act or a musical sequence. Last but not least, syncretic processing accounts for right-brain sensitivity to conditions and circumstances pertaining to an overall context or semantic field. It permits a readiness to situate signs and stimuli within a narrative setting. All the activities mentioned here require bihemispheric input, yet they manifest a preponderance of RH syncretic processing, be it visual or auditory.

While we can map them on to the two hemispheres, diacritic and syncretic functions never work in isolation from one another. Diacritic processing can hardly be obtained without some syncretic labour. Consider the difference between two kinds of watches: those that function digitally and those that

What's the difference? (drawing by Martin Blanchet)

work analogically. The LH can differentiate the two provided that the RH understands what it is exactly that unites the two objects: both are timepieces worn on the wrist. The act of discrimination presupposes a higher-level rapprochement between things that are identical in all respects save one "distinctive feature" or "differential element" (Jakobson 1985: 123, 131).

The brain can recognize differences only where objects (persons, events, etc.) have something in common. The English sound *p* differs from *b* by virtue of a phonetic convention that lumps these two sounds into a single category, namely, bilabial consonants. In linguistics the word "diacritic" thus denotes a mark used with a letter or character to distinguish it from another otherwise the same (e.g., *é* versus *è*). By definition, diacritic markings are necessarily located within fields of sameness. The argument holds true at the semantic level as well. Daytime can be distinguished from nighttime provided there is a syncretic perception of the larger unit of time known as "one day." Semiotic relations between part and whole are no exception to this rule. For instance, we can distinguish the meaning of a word appearing in a sentence provided we have information about the semantic field it belongs to, hence what unites it with other words organized into the whole sentence. A "distinct" meaning assigned to the word *pit* (is it a hole in the ground or the stone of a fruit?) hinges on all the contextual information syncretically assembled in composite acts of speech.

Syncretic processing also requires diacritic activity; measures of syncretic assemblage presuppose the supplementary work of *la différence*. Things can be identified or assimilated to one another only if there is some distance that keeps them apart. In the English language, *p* and *b* belong to the same category of bilabial consonants. This recognition of similarity makes sense as long as the difference is kept alive; otherwise effective communication may be at risk (*pit* and *bit* would no longer mean two different things). The argument applies at the semantic level. The syncretic work of metaphor is a case in point. In order to bring Christ and the lamb imagery together through metaphor (as in the Lamb slain), there must be full awareness of what separates spirit from man and man from animal. Otherwise we lose the effect of metaphor.

Unlike the word *synthesis*, the Greek term *synkretismos* conveys this paradoxical intervention of the diacritic in the syncretic; the term is simple and interactive at the same time. Originally the term denoted the union of two parties in diacritic opposition to a third; the union attempts to reduce one division yet feeds into another divide. Current usages of the English term also convey the persistence of difference within sameness. The adjective *syncretic* is typically applied to either the amalgamation of religions otherwise distinct, or a perception that fuses elements otherwise unrelated. To syncretize is thus an attempt to unite (e.g., conflicting tenets) rather than a simple eradication of difference.

The distinction between diacritic and syncretic processes offers four advantages. Firstly, it is simple in the sense of not being directly tied to composite activities such as the auditory and the visual, or the temporal and the spatial. Secondly, the distinction does not carry the legacy of some elaborate scientific or cultural perspective regarding the nature of "mental" activity. Thirdly, instead of constituting yet another rigid dyad, diacritic and syncretic processes are inherently combinative and variable. Both terms are wedded to the rule of connectivity. When mixing as they must, they generate all those matrices of "differential" (LH) and "integral" (RH) calculus that may account for the complex activities of language, music, movement, face recognition, and so on. Fourthly, these are "flexible simples" that can make sense of the concrete weavings of symbols in language, an argument we are about to explore at some length.

SEMIOTIC WEAVINGS

In the Synaptic Clefts

A few lessons can be retained from the previous discussion. To begin with, brain activity involves two "simple" processing functions, the syncretic and the diacritic. These functions may be deployed unevenly, depending on the task performed by the brain. Some operations are more syncretically oriented, while others take a diacritic slant. The two functions nonetheless work simultaneously in that they either make equal contributions to composite tasks or provide contralateral supplementation when specialization is called for. This dialogue between the two modes is embedded in definitional implications of *diakritikos* and *synkretismos*; just as a diacritic mark presupposes the sameness of two things (identical in all respects save one), so too a syncretic union of two parties entails an opposition to a third. All "mental" productions are shot through with interweavings of the global and the local, similarities and differences, efforts to unite things otherwise separate and to divide things otherwise similar. Last but not least, the two functions are "mutable simples." They combine and generate assemblages that are highly variable and malleable, which precludes any simplistic bipolar modeling of "mental" processes. Syncretic and diacritic connectivity undermines all either/or taxonomies of cognitive activity.

The same lessons should be extended to our understanding of semiosis. What can be said of lateralization in the brain can also be said of nervous signs assembled in language. Interpretive analyses applied to signs and symbols can serve to drive this argument home. For the sake of thematic unity, the examples explored in the following pages all pertain to issues of human and plant identification: that is, how proper names and plant species are constituted and manipulated through syncretic and diacritic manipulations. But first, more should be said about the parallels that lie between (1) lateral brain differences, (2) mechanisms working at the neural level, and (3) the functioning of sign connectivity. Do signs interact in ways that resemble the functioning of neurons, and can syncretic/diacritic connectivity be applied to both?

The story of the nervous system revolves around the neuron. Briefly, the central part of a neuron consists of a soma cell body surrounded by a semipermeable membrane. Neurons are in the business of transmitting signals. They do so by means of intra- and extracellular ions and a voltage differential across the cell membrane. Negatively fixed ions bathe in fluids inside the membrane. Ions endowed with a positive charge concentrate in fluids located outside. Changes in voltage across the membrane permit ions to pass through specialized single-ion membrane pores or channels, producing signal transmission from one neuron to another.

Neurons are equipped with profusions of hairy outgrowths and bushy terminals branching out to receive and transmit communicational impulses. Upstream outgrowths are called dendrites, greyish clumps of tentacles extending from the soma cell. With their help, cells receive incoming information from other neurons and pass them on via cordlike axons protruding from the soma cell. Impulses are carried away from the soma cell, into the myelinated cordlike axon, a single whitish process branching out at the terminal end and measuring from a few millimetres to a metre or more. A neuron may have anywhere from one to ten thousand axon terminals and may be stimulated by an equivalent number of neurons.

The synaptic zone (Gr. *sunapsis*, junction) is the fluid-filled area of contact between two neurons. This is where thousands

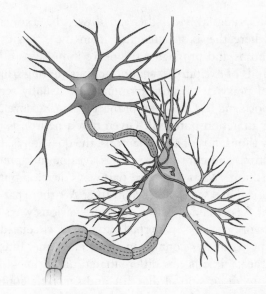

Neurons and synapses. (2nd ed., Rosenzweig, Leiman, and Breedlove, *Biological Psychology*, 32)

of signals are transmitted at various junctions in the dendritic bush and the soma cell during the space of a millisecond, resulting in multiple conversations occurring simultaneously. Synaptic impulse communication is caused by the release of chemical neurotransmitters stored in axon terminals. These chemical substances (more than one hundred currently known) affect specialized membrane sites, producing membrane events that alter the overall permeability or "resting potential" of the postsynaptic cell. Transmission occurs when the membrane is depolarized and no longer at rest. The resting (or membrane) potential of a neuron is the small electromotive force or voltage recorded across the membrane of an inactive cell and needed to equalize or polarize the electrical charges, negative and positive. When there is sufficient chemically induced current to reduce the voltage by a certain amount, then the excitable membrane is said to depolarize, causing the cell to fire and produce a large output or explosion. The depolarizing impulse or "action potential" will then go down the axon from the hillock (where the axon emanates from the soma cell) to its terminal bulbs and propagate the nerve impulse to other cells.

Thousands of excitatory synaptic actions coming from a great number of presynaptic axon terminals are usually required to bring a postsynaptic cell membrane to a firing level, thereby triggering an action potential. Given that a neuron is normally excited by thousands of other neurons, the question is: How will these multiple and contradictory messages be interpreted in an orderly fashion? What regulated pathways develop out of these densely reticulated webs of neural traffic? Are there paths within the jungle? As explained below, there are various ways in which neural networking can be patterned into orderly circuits, depending on how the pathways connect in space and time. Interestingly, some of these circuits are differentiated along lines that echo our previous discussion of diacritic and syncretic connectivity.

First of all, a distinction can be made between simple-consecutive networking and networking involving parallel routes. While the former involves a neural-chain system that tends to be predictable (as in sensory-motor reflex activity), the latter generates processing activities that occur simultaneously and with some relative autonomy (as when synchronizing song and body movement). The distinction can be applied to a comparison between chemical and electrical forms of neural conversations. Chemical events entail synaptic connections that proceed sequentially, through the release of chemical neurotransmitters and resulting changes in membrane permeability. While they allow variations in amplitude, these connections produce a delay between synaptic activities and the onset of postsynaptic potentials. As a result, communications tend to be slow. By contrast, direct electrical connections between adjacent cell membranes occur between cells that fire simultaneously. This produces parallel neural activity and rhythmic patterns that are essential for sensorimotor coordination and synchronicity and for embryonic nervous tissue growth as well. Note that myelin, a white fatty substance forming the medullary sheath of certain nerve fibres, plays an important role in providing electrical insulation between neurons and increasing the transmission speed of electrical impulses.

In short, the brain functions step by step, through diacritic time sequences. But it also functions syncretically, as "a massively parallel information-processing system," displaying synchronous activity governed by principles of efficiency and economy. Not everything can be done "by millions of steps arranged in sequence. There is simply not enough time" (Churchland 1986: 35, 137).

Secondly, some configurations follow divergent routes, with several connections transmitting a signal originating from a common neural area. An instance of this would be information sent by the optic nerve to different regions of the cortex, or a visual stimulus causing multiple reactions such as head movement, memories, and verbalization. Other networks follow a convergent pattern, all signals being directed towards a central area. For example, a multitude of signals received by visual receptor cells are brought together in eye ganglion cells. Visual, auditory, and tactile stimuli converging on a particular emotion is another example. It should be emphasized that divergent and convergent communications are not mutually exclusive. They can be combined, as when multiple neurons converge on a smaller nerve area that in turn stimulates several regions of brain activity. The convergence of visual input followed by divergent output to the cortex is a case in point. Note also that divergent and convergent circuits require both sequential and parallel activities. With divergent events, fewer concurrent nerve connections are sequentially followed by a greater number of connections operating simultaneously. With convergence the sequence is simply reversed.

The production and propagation of impulses is what the nervous system is all about. Cells and neurons are distinguishable units of living tissue. But their principal task is to network with other cells and neurons through synaptic exchanges, depolarizations and action potentials, forming reticular patterns and circuits that may be sequential or parallel, divergent or convergent.

Signs in language are no different. They too are distinguishable units that can branch out in multiple directions, using the variegated "processes" (activities and outgrowths) of language to connect with other sign-cells of the nervous sign system. But can the neural analogy help us in making sense of the dense arborization of sign connections? Can "neurosemiosis" explain what goes on in those synaptic interspaces or clefts that separate one "soma sign" from another?

These questions can be partly answered by making a distinction between two types of "signaptic events": syncretic ones (RH) implicating the convergence of sign-cells otherwise distal, and diacritic ones (LH) implicating the divergence of signs otherwise proximate. While both events are "sign action potentials" or depolarizations that produce active sign communications, they generate distinct patterns that may be unevenly deployed from one semiotic context to another.

In the analyses to follow, we shall see that some scripts may accentuate principles of centripetal-convergent mediation. Others may be dominated by the centrifugal-divergent mode. As with the brain lateralization phenomenon, however, I argue that each mode consistently requires supplementary firings from the nondominant mode. There is no convergent connectivity without the works of divergence, and vice versa. The end result is what we might call an analogic deployment of the action potentials of language. Semiosis can never be reduced to a digital application of rules of convergence and divergence, with all of one meaning none of the other, as in binary systems of computation. Rather, the relationship between syncretic and diacritic operations is essentially a matter of degree or amplitude.

Convergence never occurs in the absolute, with a centripetal fusion of sign-cells that become so closely mediated through metaphor or other means that their differences and polarities can be fully extinguished. The opposite is also true. Signs are never so divisive as to create digitalities cast in stone (e.g., mind versus matter) or a chaotic sliding constantly drifting away from centres of semiotic gravity. Just as metaphors play themselves out through webs of differences, so too oppositions and digressions proceed through pathways and fields delimited by the conventions of language and culture. Sign processing plays on the gaps and proximities that lie between signs, without ever doing away with either gaps or proximities. What can be said of differences intertwining with similarities can also be said of parts interacting with the whole. The nervous sign system is bilateralized in the sense of involving constant movements between parts and whole, with variable attention being paid to meaningful fragments and configurations of sign production. All in all, nervous sign activity is both centrifugal and centripetal, both divergent and convergent, with a constant interfacing of diacritic detail and syncretic perspective.

Before I say more on the absorbing subject of neurosemiotics, a few precautionary notes regarding parallels between semiosis and neural activity should be made. One thing I am not advancing is the contentious "grandmother cell" hypothesis: that is, the notion that there are high-level cells or cell assemblages responding to the presence of precise stimuli (Barlow 1972). We do not know enough about the brain to make any intelligent claim about the exact ways in which neural activity translates into language and sign expressions. A simple stimulus, say, the sound of a church bell, can generate the electrical activation of thousands of cells working together and in different areas of the brain, adding up to an event-related potential (ERP) that can be recorded at the surface of the skull or within the brain. Measurements of ERPs give us a useful but nonetheless vague idea of how vast populations of neurons interact. The precise relationship that lies between the sign compositions of language and aggregate action potentials ordered simultaneously and sequentially still remains a mystery.

Nor am I proposing that semiotics simply borrow and emulate the language of neuropsychology. What I am suggesting is that signs will connect in ways that have neurological foundations and are likely to resemble neural communications. After all, sign actions are products of the brain. Since this statement may still be read as an invitation to neurobiological reductionism, I should point out that semiotics and philosophy have much to offer and can play a leading role in rethinking the findings of neuroscience. Theories of signification can provide crucial insights into how brain products actually function, over and beyond the digital modelling of cognitive activity often prevailing in neuropsychology. Though subject to debate, knowledge we have concerning language and symbolling can feed back into discussions of brain activity. Among other things, interpretations of sign activity and related theories of language can shed considerable light on complex phenomena such as variations in amplitudes of syncretic and diacritic connectivity.

On this last point I should warn readers that I will not reduce sign networking to variable configurations of acts of RH convergence and LH divergence. Principles that involve factors such as attentionality, emotionality, and memory will have to be taken into consideration and serve to qualify and revise models developed in this book. Accordingly, discussions of axial issues of affect and judgment will be addressed in *The 3-D Mind* 2; questions of memory and anticipation governing the coronal plane, in *The 3-D Mind* 3. In this book I concentrate on "neurosemiotic" parallels mapped along the sagittal plane. Interpretive analyses that follow focus on connections of the syncretic and diacritic kind, with an emphasis on convergent and divergent communications in space *but not in time*. As already pointed out, diacritic processing often proceeds sequentially, that is, doing things one after the other. Diacritic activity, however, can be generated without the intervention of time series. While the word "bittersweet" places bitterness before sweetness, the two signs can be part of a diacritic opposition expressed without sequentiality; bitterness is then simply the opposite of sweetness (beer and sugar don't mix well). For the moment we bracket the time factor in language and do so as if signification occurred in synchrony alone.

The four analyses to follow illustrate how signs reticulate through webs of similarities and differences, mediations and separations. Nervous signs in action involve a playful manipulation of centripetal and centrifugal forces in language. In reticle 7, I begin this demonstration with an instance of "literal denotation and identification" representing syncretic processing at its height: namely, a proper name, my own, apparently undivided from within and firmly wired to a particular individual. The question is whether or not this act of naming can be understood as a "simple" representation that can be activated without any trace of divisive circuitry. Does "Jacques M. Chevalier" entail a straightforward connection between a single sign action and a single person, as opposed to a complex "signaptic" event playing on both the gaps and proximities of sign reticles?

Although more complex, the second example (reticle 8) is also characterized by a dominance of syncretic activity. It consists of a line of poetry taken from Longfellow's *Evangeline*, a line offering signs of continuity conveyed through botanical imagery (forest, pines, and hemlocks). The question that this poetry raises is similar to the one raised in my analysis of naming practices: can a gestalt tone of harmony dispense with supplementary notes of diacritical opposition?

The third and fourth interpretive examples have botanical overtones as well and are taken from myths of biblical and native Mexican origins. Unlike the preceding material, however, both compositions follow divergent strategies, deploying signs that emphasize divisions and discontinuities in the narrative realm. The biblical material (reticle 9) is from the Book of Genesis and revolves around the fig apron motif, a reminder of the fall of Adam and Eve and the rupture that separates the human condition from life in Eden. The last example (reticle 10) explores an even clearer illustration of diacritic "thinking" expressed through a primordial duel pitting hero against foe. The myth in question narrates the confrontation of a Mexican Gulf Nahua divinity and his animal predator, the corn god and the iguana. The central question in both analyses concerns the supplementary input of *synkretismos* in sign activities otherwise ruled by the logic of *diakritikos*. Can mythology draw attention to gaps in the suture while ignoring stitches in the joint?

What's in a Name?

Can language be purely literal? Can we use terms that are strictly denotative, like fingers that point to objects? Do words act like sound tags that we assign to phenomena perceived or experienced through the senses? Isn't language all about this syncretic fusion of word elements and elements of the world, one-to-one linkages enabling us to communicate information about phenomena through words designed to represent them?

We normally use language without asking these questions. We assume that it is in our power to generate referential words that are so simple to use as to preclude complex mappings of sign connections. Of all words available in European languages, nouns are good examples of these referential name-tags, each signifying something through an arbitrary sound-image standing for a particular object, subject, or event. Common nouns, however, are not perfect illustrations of literal name-tags. They designate not unique things but rather objects that share common denominators demarcating them from other similar objects. The word *cat* thus denotes all members of the species *as distinct* from other pet animals such as dogs. Common nouns represent determinate classes based on *distinctive commonalties* that the brain can apprehend through combined syncretic and diacritic "thinking" – perceiving similarities that cats share and that separate them from other domestic animals.

Proper nouns provide perhaps a better example of what denotations do. Each proper noun designates a single person,

Jacques M. Chevalier

place, etc., with unique characteristics not shared by anything or anyone else. Each proper name is an "unflexible simple," as it were. Consider the name appearing on the cover of this book, Jacques M. Chevalier. To my knowledge, this full name belongs to the author and no one else. The name is a word group by which the author as an individual can be "properly" introduced, identified, spoken to, and spoken of. It serves as a sign of his "self," simply naming him, signalling his unique identity, as opposed to representing a class of people or implying a set of qualities exclusively shared by those of the same kind. Like other proper names, Jacques M. Chevalier is not a full grammatical sentence consisting of component parts that add up to a meaningful language composition, with a subject, adjectives, articles, prepositions, adverbs, and complements. Rather, it is a single name converging on a selfsame person, an individual human being neither divisible nor separable, someone existing as a singular and separate being, "one of a kind," so to speak.

This is how proper names are culturally perceived. Common nouns can emulate them through the use of adjectives, verbs, and adverbs that serve to specify unique individuals within a class, like a cat existing in the *hic et nun* ("the black cat I own and which you saw at my house last week"). But the denotative virtues of proper names are by no means obvious. Although apparently "simple" and uncompounded, proper names are products of language requiring sophisticated sign-processing activity. When known to the subject, proper names can be retrieved in no time and without effort. Yet the background operations that go into producing and understanding what the name signifies are multiple and complex. They involve a composite mapping of similarities and differences that are indispensable to all acts of "proper naming." No one can make sense of the Jacques M. Chevalier inscription appearing on the cover of this book without having prior knowledge of the proper naming system that gave this author his name. The rules in question convey information regarding gender, family affiliation, cultural background, and so on. Readers and listeners can extract information from this name on condition that they are familiar with the conventions involved. Among other things, they must be able to recognize:

- proper nouns as distinct from common nouns; the former are marked with capital letters (as opposed to lower-case letters) when put in writing and they often have no intrinsic signification (other than original meanings that tend to go unremembered; e.g., Jacques is from Heb. *ya'aqob*, Jacob, literally, seizing by the heel, hence a supplanter);
- masculine names as distinct from feminine names;
- the surname normally ascribed to a person through biological connections, from father to child, as distinct from the first name, also known as the Christian name; the latter is the "first name" deliberately chosen by the parents and "given" to the child soon after birth, possibly on the occasion of a baptismal ceremony (with the assistance of godparents), to be used without the surname to indicate informality or familiarity;

- names suggesting French origin and/or mother tongue as distinct from other linguistic backgrounds;
- specific historical trends in name giving – e.g., French-speaking Catholic baby boomers "christening" their children with names of saints and the apostles, including Jacques;
- signs of intellectual property conveyed through proper names attached to books.

Given these naming conventions, it would be logical to assume that the Jacques M. Chevalier signature converges on a male adult of French origin and/or mother tongue whose father's family name was Chevalier. One could also surmise that he is a member of the baby-boomer generation, someone born at a time when names of the apostles such as Jacques (or Pierre, Jean, or Paul – his three actual brothers) were in vogue. Given these circumstances, one could hypothesize that the name Jacques was given to this individual shortly after birth, possibly at baptism. Finally, our signature conventions being what they are, it would make sense to assume that Jacques M. Chevalier has authored the books entitled *The 3-D Mind* bearing his name.

A simple name tells a story. Far from being mere pointers or name-tags resulting in the simple convergence or "coordination of two objects" (Heidegger 1968: 120), proper names locate people within networks of signification, fitting them into distinctive categories and classes established by semantic convention. The name I chose by way of illustration (and whose interpretation someone else could have signed) points to a human being, an adult, male, Christian, French-speaking baby-boomer, the son of a man named Chevalier, and the author of a book. But proper names not only locate subjects within webs of meaningful positions; they also introduce webs of signification within subjects. That is, they mark the limits of proper name identities and introduce signs of plurality and divergence within the order of selfsameness.

Proper names do not merely identify; they also circumscribe the choices and selective limits of individuality. All of the attributes attached to the Jacques M. Chevalier signature are

markers of individuality that preclude other attributes not
deemed appropriate markers of proper identity. Signs of culturally preferred patrilineality embedded in the family name are a
case in point: Jacques M. Chevalier's name is without a mat-
ronym, in keeping with existing conventions. The matrilineal
bond is ignored. Paradoxically, signs of identity are selective
and partial. They evoke some attributes of the whole person
but not all of what makes up the indivisible subject.

Our proper naming system also inscribes divergences within
the selfsame subject. Whether they are conscious of this or not,
persons customarily known by their Christian names and biological patronyms are bearers of a dualism inspired by the Judeo-
Christian tradition: to be more precise, the division between the
worldly (legal-biological) and the otherworldly (spiritual). Our
names are constant reminders of the distance that lies between
two principles of personal identity construction. On the one
hand, through the patronym a formal-legal and biological connection is established between father and child. On the other
hand, the given name may be used to convey everything that a
Christian name is meant to signify – traditionally, the child's
accession to the life and fellowship of the spirit (at baptism).
Alternatively, the first name can be used to specify a *distinct*
individual within a family. It may also indicate informality and
familiarity (as distinct from formality and legality), hence a sec-
ularized version of human fellowship. Be that as it may, the
proper name serves to write a formative "moitie system" into
each person's apparently undivided selfhood, decomposing it
into its component parts conceived in a western perspective.

Note that this Jacques is also christened Joseph Louis Allyre,
a threefold name that appears before his first name on some
legal documents but not on the signature of this book. While
they convey signs of diacritic uniqueness (surely no other person
is named Joseph Louis Allyre Jacques Chevalier!), the three
names also carry meanings that fall somewhere between Christian
names and family surnames. That is, they create a plane of
convergence, a middle-ground naming code that conjoins signs
of Christian spirituality with indices of biological filiation (in

this case between father and son): more specifically, Joseph is the father of Christ, a proper name assigned to all male followers of Christ; Louis is the name of the godfather who attended Jacques's baptismal ceremony; and Allyre is the name of the priestly father who performed the ritual. All three surnames are signatures of *spiritual fatherhood and emulation* – religiously inspired and patrilineal at the same time. These are conventional signs of a syncretic effort to bring together things otherwise separate (spirituality and biology).

The naming conventions discussed above are by no means universal, not even within western culture or history. A straightforward patronymic rule does not prevail in Spanish-speaking countries. In Iceland, people inherit their father's given name, not the family name. Historically, modern English surnames became common practice only in the late Middle Ages, a time when they started being used to establish legal distinctions among members of the propertied classes. Unlike current English surnames, family names were used to indicate the person's patrilateral ancestry (Stevenson, son of Steven) but also attributions of appearance or manner (Brown, Russell), or the person's occupation (Smith) or place of residence (Moore, York). In ancient Rome, a person's name was assembled along different lines. It included a personal forename (praenomen), a clan or gens name (nomen; Caius Julius Caesar was of the Julian clan), a family name (cognomen), and sometimes an agnomen honouring a particular exploit or event. Naming practices also change through history and are still undergoing transformations. The rule that a married woman assumes her husband's surname at marriage and does not transmit her "maiden name" to her own children is now widely challenged.

In short, it is only in a very limited sense that Jacques M. Chevalier's name is "his own," like a literal word denotation or personalized totem (Lévi-Strauss 1962: 285) that belongs to no one else and that he only can truly "sign." In reality, this author's name is the product of a particular name-sign system designed to register reticles of similarities and differences, signature conventions that are still undergoing transformations and that diverge from naming systems used in previous eras and other cultures. While the brain can make a direct connection between a book title and an author's name, it can do so only with background knowledge of these rules built into this name and others of the same class. As soon as the Jacques M. Chevalier inscription is spotted on the book cover, the informed reader enters a semantic field involving a particular perspective on the relationship between words, humans, and things (the name connects an owning subject with his thing-like property). Far from being a mere denotation, the name-tag is a window that opens on to a proper-naming perspective centred on particular notions of identity, individuality, gendering, christening, patronymic biology, linguistic affiliation, intellectual property, and so on.

No word can exist without dwelling in language. Words that "simply denote" are like nerve cells without axons, dendrites, axon terminals, synapse, and connections to other cells. If they do not reticulate, they are without life. Signs come alive only when activated within broader networks of sign connections generated through weavings of similarities and differences. Each sign is merely a stitch in a broader fabric of syncretic proximities and diacritic gaps.

Sign interchanges resemble communications that go on in the gap that separates one neuron from another, the synaptic zone. Neurons have soma cells that branch out and interconnect through processes known as dendrites, axons, and axon terminals. The same can be said of signs. They are units of meaning that are inherently communicative and interactive, generating variable interconnections obtained through a dense fabric of sign processes (grammatical, metaphorical, colloquial, etc.). The synaptic *distance and linkage* established between two "word-cells" such as *Jacques* and *Chevalier* are a case in point. While the two words could have gone in different directions, associating themselves with other signs (as in "a Jacquerie revolt," "a chevalier of industry," etc.), their actual combination offers one permissible connection that can play an informative role given the appropriate context, for example, attaching a particular name to a particular book.

From a linguistic perspective, the J.C. assemblage brings together two sets of "signaptic" action potentials mapped on to lines of convergence and divergence. On the one hand, the J.C. association presupposes a syncretism of two proper names, Christian and patronymic, both of which converge on a single person. The assemblage is the end result of a naming action that proceeds through semantic pathways linking higher-order categorizations to lower-class specifications. The name is the arrival point of a logical journey that proceeds from the use of words of French origin to nouns within it, proper nouns, to be more precise, those applied to human beings and to one particular family and a single individual within it. This syncretism of multiple pieces and levels of information converges on a simple task, which consists in naming a person.

On the other hand, signs of a naming system can be connected only if proper distinctions are registered and remain operative throughout the act of naming and the enforcement of related conventions. The ability to distinguish is so vital to the act of proper naming that the convergence effect can never be absolute. The brain will make sense of the Jacques M. Chevalier signature provided it is able to grasp the distance that separates patronyms from Christian names, humans from non-humans, proper nouns from common nouns, nouns from verbs, French from other European languages, and so on. For someone's composite name to be recognized, knowledge of the differences that lie between orders of classification and levels of generality must be acquired. For instance, the rule according to which proper names are to be treated as a sub-field within the broader field of nouns must be operative. The brain is obliged to register conventional differences between field and sub-fields if it is to make sense of the simplest acts of language. Given its focus on distinctions and contrasts, the plane of divergence keeps track of these critical distances that lie between elements within a field and between levels of classification as well.

To sum up, "sign cells" interact in two ways that are mutually interdependent. Sign action potentials require syncretic associations between signs brought together within appropriate fields of sameness or likeness. But sign impulses also require diacritic knowledge of contrasts and differences. Connections of the first kind never do without reticles of the second kind (and vice versa), not even in the most elementary expressions of language. Proper names illustrate this point. Although commonly viewed as denotative name-tags that simply point to subjects and their selfsame identities, proper names presuppose divisive processes that break down subjects into their component parts and assign them precise locations within systems of differential classification. Proper names may bring together component parts of the subject and elements within logically related fields. All the same, it is not in their power (or interest!) to fully bridge these distances by dissolving all gaps and crevices in language.

Signs are always in the middle of other signs. Middle names are a good reminder of that. This brings us to a telling "M." standing in (and for?) the middleness of Jacques M. Chevalier. The diacritic function of this initial is almost obvious: once again, no one else is likely to be called by this name. Unlike the Joseph Louis Allyre triad, however, the M. marker goes off into directions that diverge from familiar grounds. That is, the middle initial names a departure from conventional ways. The letter M has been voluntarily added and inserted to signify the mother's surname (Molleur), thereby choosing to introduce matrilineality where there was none. The alteration reflects a convention borrowed from the English naming system, introducing a middle-naming practice relatively foreign to the French. When understood in context, the deviation points to broader cultural transformations involving new relations between genders (read the influence of feminism) and between cultures as well (read the effects of anglicization). This is a case of signs of divergence playing themselves out in the middle of something new.

The Forest Primeval

A person's name is a relatively simple composition. But what about more complex acts of signification – will the same argument hold? Is it truly the case that "signaptic" distances can never be fully annulled? Can we not argue that right-brain processes are well equipped to mend a world fragmented by left-brain thinking? In semiotic parlance, could we not argue that *metaphors and words of poetic mediation* offer harmonic measures to attenuate or even eradicate the divisive effects of linear thinking and the analytic mind?

A concrete example is in order. Consider the following line of poetry, from Longfellow's once-celebrated *Evangeline*, first published in 1847:

> This is the forest primeval. The murmuring pines
> and the hemlocks

The words are from the prologue of Longfellow's poem, introducing a tale of paradise lost *à l'Acadienne*, a romantic rewriting of Edenic imagery in the light of New World history. The story told is that of the Fall without sin, as exemplified by the deportation of Acadians by the British in 1755. The fate of Acadie is embodied in the sufferings of the saintly maiden of Grand-Pré, separated from her lover while in exile (Chevalier 1990).

Let the analysis begin on the plane of convergence. In Longfellow's forest primeval imagery, readers can detect a mood of timeless harmony and spatial continuity. The material creates a scene of temporal harmony by establishing a relationship of complete identity ("this is") between an ahistoric present and the origin of time. This aesthetic effect of near-immortality is reinforced by the evocation of evergreen trees impervious to seasonal oscillations between life and death-like dormancy. To this prevailing mood of durability can be added the production of continuous "murmuring" sound. Harmony is achieved on the spatial plane as well, by means of an uncomplicated motif of tall, excurrent pine growth uniting heaven and earth. Lastly, the evocation of "pines and hemlocks" points to the rule of botanical unity in diversity; the American hemlock belongs to the genus *Tsuga* of the pine family.

As with the Jacques M. Chevalier signature, associations of the forest primeval imagery generate impressions of *sameness*, *homogeneity*, and *identity*. Unlike an act of proper naming, however, Longfellow's opening line fosters a particular mood. Sentiments of primitive naturalism coupled with evocations of everlasting unity prevail. When read from a neuropsychological perspective, this material seems to appeal to the RH, which specializes in processing emotions and relations in space, as opposed to divisions in logic and time.

Right-brain activity triggered by the opening words of *Evangeline* is reinforced by effects of rhythmic musicality and mournful prosody obtained through the metrical arrangements. The poem is an exercise in hexametric prosody. We know that Longfellow's decision to use the hexameter was directly influenced by his reading of Greek and Latin classics, Tegnér's *The Children of the Lord's Supper*, and Goethe's *Hermann und Dorothea*, this last a drama resembling the Acadian Diaspora and revolving around the history of Protestants exiled from Salzburg. Poems written in this elegiac form are typically associated with the mournfully contemplative tone of lament and praise for the dead. *Evangeline's* dactylic hexameter lends itself to a slow-paced, melancholic composition in a minor key that borders on effects of plaintive monotony.

The English version of the dactylic hexameter contains six metrical feet or measures, with variable combinations of dactyls

Hemlock by the ocean (drawing by Martin Blanchet)

(one accented syllable followed by two unaccented), trochees (one accented syllable followed by one unaccented) and spondees (two accented syllables). As shown below, *Evangeline*'s first line is a simple version of the hexametric form consisting of five dactyls followed by a spondee.

In keeping with a narrative that laments another lost paradise, effects of mournful tonality are secured through a rising

1	2	3	4	5	6
dactyl	dactyl	dactyl	dactyl	dactyl	spondee
(´ - -)	(´ - -)	(´ - -)	(´ - -)	(´ - -)	(´ ´)

This is the / forest prim / eval. The / murmuring / pines and the / hemlocks

and falling tone flowing in a monotonous cadence. The plaintive elegy of bygone days calls for dactylic verses that produce a singsong heartbeat effect, fading away with the murmuring of the last syllable.

Other metric arrangements involving the same imagery would not have produced the same results. The subject matter of *Evangeline* precludes flights of passionate imagination and terse lines of heroism as well. To prove the latter point, Longfellow converted the passage on the mockingbird song (part 2, canto 2) into heroic measures of pentameter couplets.

In the original hexametric version, the variations in the length of each line of verse (up to seventeen syllables) are conducive to a narrative description unhampered by measures of prosodic restraint:

> Then from a neighbouring thicket the mocking-bird,
>   wildest of singers,
> Swinging aloft on a willow spray that hung o'er the water,
> Shook from his little throat such floods of delirious music,
> That the whole air and the woods and the waves
>   seemed silent to listen.
> Plaintive at first were the tones and sad: then soaring
>   to madness
> Seemed they to follow or guide the revel of frenzied
>   Bacchantes.
> Single notes were then heard, in sorrowful, low
>   lamentation;
> Till, having gathered them all, he flung them abroad
>   in derision,
> As when, after a storm, a gust of wind through the
>   tree-tops
> Shakes down the rattling rain in a crystal shower on
>   the branches.

Note the lingering quality of the mockingbird song and the losses suffered in the rhymed pentameter translation suggested by Longfellow (over page). Moreover, while highly repetitive, the hexametric rhythm shows variations based on the ratio of

dactyls to spondees (and trochees). Excessive monotony is offset
by changes in the location of the caesura as well; in Greek and
Latin verse, the caesura falls within the metrical foot, while in
English verse the break usually comes at about the middle of
the line. Finally, the sheer length of the hexameter calls for a
pause at the end of each verse; the break comes naturally to
readers pausing for breath as they follow a long-winded narrative bordering on prose. The tale of Acadie reads as prose
gone softly melodic and rhythmic.

The five-foot, iambic translation in rhymes is a terse parody
of the original hexametric passage:

> Upon a spray that overhung the stream,
> The mocking-bird, awaking from his dream,
> Poured such delirious music from his throat
> That all the air seemed listening to his note.
> Plaintive at first the song began, and slow;
> It breathed of sadness, and of pain and woe;
> Then, gathering all his notes, abroad he flung
> The multitudinous music from his tongue, –
> As, after showers, a sudden gust again
> Upon the leaves shakes down the rattling rain.

The metre chosen by Longfellow was meant to flow naturally.
By concerning himself with the detailed metrical corrections
suggested by his friend Felton, Longfellow achieved the natural
flow of a prosody filled with mournful musicality. To para-
phrase the author, while *Evangeline* was hard to write, the final
text was easy to read. The poet invested technical effort into
harmonizing rhythm with accent and quantity, producing "a
poem which many people take for prose," as opposed to "a prose
tale, which many people would have taken for poetry" (cf.
Hawthorne and Longfellow 1947: 40).

Signs of unity in time and space, mixed with accents of
melodic melancholia, all point to cognitive processes typical of
RH. *Evangeline*'s opening line is mapped onto reticles of convergence, a plane known for its sensitivity to coordinates in
space (as opposed to divisions in time) and to expressions of

emotionality, tonality, and musicality. When unassisted by the left brain, the RH shows signs of depression and sadness, effects also deployed in the poetry examined above. Lastly, RH processing shows little concern for grammatical conventions, distorting the usual sequencing of words possibly with emotional intent. In *Evangeline* the "primeval forest" motif thus becomes the "forest primeval."

Does this mean that Longfellow's poem speaks mostly to syncretistic inclinations of the RH? Not exactly. As with all productions of language, bihemispheric activity is essential for poets and readers to process intricate imageries and related affects. The forest primeval composition is no exception to this rule. For one thing, the LH plays a critical role in reading and writing. Moreover, as with music, poetry requires complex measurements. Although resulting in a melodic text that flows naturally and may be easy to read, the meticulous effort that Longfellow put into writing hexametric lines called for left-brain expertise in the use of language and the application of rules and conventions of poetry.

On the semantic level, a poem will produce indices of harmony and unity on condition that analytic differences requiring mediation be duly signified. "This is the forest primeval" may evoke continuity through time, yet the phrase does not extinguish the distinction that lies between the distant past and the immediate present, or the actual text being read ("this is") and the remote "forest primeval" that comes immediately after. While the imagery works at bridging distances in time and space, these distances are by no means fully annulled.

The same argument applies to musical effects built into Longfellow's composition. They too involve some diacritic activity. Hexametric prosody requires that tonal differences be sustained throughout the poem. However monotonous the metrical arrangements may be, distinctions between accented and unaccented syllables must be repeated line after line if the composition is to generate the intended rhythm and resulting mood. Pauses involving a moving caesura and shifts between meters, dactyls, spondees, and trochees also represent minimal discontinuities that the poem must iterate verse after verse to produce the desired effect.

Last but not least, the mournful mood created by the forest primeval scenery (and the saddening imageries of *Evangeline*) is a constant reminder of a fundamental rupture in time. The past *is no longer*, and the Golden Age of Acadie is merely a memory. The tale of Acadie is a prosodic expression of melancholia harking back to the blessings of heaven on earth. This mournful effect is embedded in the constant launching and termination of hexametric verses; pauses between meters and in the middle and at the end of each line; alternations between accented and unaccented syllables fitting into dactyls, spondees, and trochees. Note also that in the primeval forest scenery, rupture in time is given the last word, via a doubly accented spondee (*hém-lócks*) that brings the rhythmic continuity of this elegiac line to a sudden end. Hemlocks create a rupture in the prosodic measurement of time, a "final end" that conveys the lamenting of Acadie through a closure of dactylic melody.

Signs of divergent times and spaces can be detected at the semantic level as well. Consider the botanical expression of the immortality theme, which is not as straightforward as it may seem. Pines are the epitome of long-lasting life. The same cannot be said of the hemlock motif, which happens to be responsible for putting an end to *Evangeline*'s first line. Hemlocks are of the pine family, yet in Europe the word generally designates a poisonous weed of the carrot family, or the conium, known to have caused the death of Socrates. In spatial terms, we are faced with severe limitations on effects of vertical mediation. Trees may grow tall but they never leave the ground (unlike other mediators such as birds). More importantly, hemlocks have drooping branches and are also associated with weeds, plants with no upward growth. Finally, murmuring sounds are by no means reassuring. Like poisonous weeds, murmurings are usually kept low. Moreover, they can be used to kill the rhythm of vocal life through effects of plaintive monotony or dissonant grumbling.

The primeval forest scene mingles expressions of harmony with negative developments approaching the surface narrative.

The hemlock motif evoked in the prologue is a harmonic mediator, a "tall evergreen" that reduces the distance between heaven and earth, the past and the present. Yet its homonymic association with the poisonous weed of the carrot family imposes severe limitations on what this sign can do to resolve oppositions in time and space.

Of all motifs appearing in the forest primeval imagery, the word "hemlock" can be singled out for the bitterness of its tone. Briefly, when located in its broader cultural context, the poem's hemlock motif is a transmutation of the biblical gall and wormwood. In the scriptures, "gall" means either bile or the acrid plant offered to Christ on the cross. As for wormwood (*Artemisia*), it designates any of several species of bitter plants that usually grow in the desert. That the hemlock should be assigned negative attributes is confirmed by many scriptural expressions, such as:

- the fruit of integrity turning into gall or growing as hemlock in the furrows of the field;
- disobedient men prone to temptations of "green envy" – men who resemble roots that bear gall and wormwood and are likened to serpents whose poisonous sting was thought to contain venom from the animal's gall;
- God punishing the wicked by pouring their gall on the ground, or giving them wormwood and gall for food;
- the wormwood that spoils the many waters of whorish Babylon sinking into the sea or the deep at the end of time; and
- a bitter life that is wormwood to man.[5]

To conclude this analysis, a close reading of *Evangeline*'s first line illustrates a basic point: syncretic lines drawn on the plane of convergence require contralateral supplementation of the divergent sort. Readers of poetry can apprehend harmonic coordinates in time and space, provided they are informed of all those divisions and differences that stand in need of mediation and reconciliation. This is to say that RH effects of logical mediation or gestalt unity can never be achieved in the absolute,

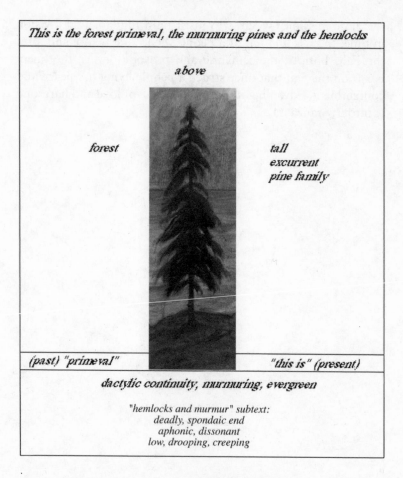

This is the forest primeval, the murmuring pines and the hemlocks

above

forest

tall
excurrent
pine family

(past) "primeval"   *"this is" (present)*

dactylic continuity, murmuring, evergreen

"hemlocks and murmur" subtext:
deadly, spondaic end
aphonic, dissonant
low, drooping, creeping

without leaving some trace of the gaps and crevices that need attenuation. Similar comments apply to the right-brain inclination to repetition, monotony, and melancholy. Rather than implying LH inactivity, signs of grief, mourning, and depression can be foregrounded, provided there are breaks in language to signify the ruptures that are causing sorrow in the first place.

In *Evangeline* discontinuity is registered through speech sounds constantly rising and falling, a two-tone variation typically moving from one accented to two unaccented syllables. The resulting speech medium is in keeping with the poem's semantic mission, which is to insist on a fundamental division in time: the *rise and fall* of a people, hence life before and after the Fall. Both at the semantic and prosodic levels, the poem harps on the Fall that once struck a people living in "peace and contentment," dwelling in the Golden Age of love and harmony (canto 1, stanza 1).

Who Gives a Fig?

Lines of convergence and divergence crisscross in variable ways. Among other things, they are subject to variations in levels of mediation. The work of mediation ranges from effects of harmony verging on monotony to admissions of fragmentation and outright discord. Most acts of speech fall somewhere between these two extremes. That is, most reticles of language will incorporate activity from both planes, with one set of "mental" processes possibly playing a dominant position and the other a function of necessary supplementarity. Line 1 of *Evangeline* is an example of predominant indices of mediation and convergence, coupled with sub-indices of dualities recurring in time and space.

We now turn to the opposite scenario, which consists in clear expressions of splits and crevices in the world, with few concessions to remedies of mediation and the restoration of unity. While related again to imageries of the Fall and botanical expressions thereof, the example discussed below is from a different and much older source: the Book of Genesis, chapter 3. It reads as follows:

And the serpent said unto the woman, Ye shall not surely die: For God doth know that in the day ye eat thereof, then your eyes shall be opened, and ye shall be as gods, knowing good and evil. And when the woman saw that the tree was good for food, and that it was pleasant to the eyes, and a tree to be desired to make one wise, she took of the fruit thereof, and did eat, and gave also unto her husband with her; and he did eat. And the eyes of them both were opened, and they knew that they were naked; and they sewed *fig leaves* together, and made themselves aprons. And they heard the voice of the Lord God walking in the garden in the cool of the day: and Adam and his wife hid themselves from the presence of the Lord God amongst the trees of the garden (Gen. 3.4–8).

Because they ate the fruit of the knowledge of good and evil, man and woman were compelled to hide their shameful nudity behind leaves of the fig tree. Thus began the story of the human condition as we know it.

Why the fig leaves to mark the greatest rupture of all, as conceived in a Judeo-Christian perspective? The answer lies in themes written all over Genesis 3, themes that harness the fig motif to the tribulations of life on earth after the Fall. The trials in question involve incompatibilities between life and death, man and woman, pain and pleasure – diacritic oppositions deeply inscribed in the fig imagery. A well-known characteristic of edible fig trees such as *Ficus carica* consists of a reproductive affliction, namely, self-sterility. This is the species's inability to fertilize itself with its own pollen. The affliction generates a rather complex sex life for the species, knowledge of which was and is still indispensable to fig subsistence culture.

The *Ficus carica* has two forms, the common female fig tree and the male caprifig. The common fig has no viable male flowers. But it has numerous long-style, female flowers located inside the syconium, the fleshy receptacle that eventually turns into the edible fruit. By contrast, the caprifig yields inedible fruits and has numerous male flowers that contain pollen. The caprifig also has short-styled female flowers or galls that house the larva of an insect known as the fig wasp (*Blastophaga psenes*). Some eggs and larvae growing inside caprifig fruits develop into male wasps that eventually eat their way into galls and mate with the females. Female wasps will then break out of the caprifig fruits through the syconium opening called the "ostiole," covering themselves with pollen from the nearby male flowers. This occurs at the time of the "profichi" caprifig

God the Father reproaching Adam and Eve. Limbourg Brothers (15th c.).
Detail of the Expulsion from Paradise (lower right). Illuminated miniature
from the Tres Riches Heures du Duc de Berry. 1416. Ms. 65, f.25 verso.
Musée Conde, Chantilly, France. Photo: R.G. Ojeda. Copyright Réunion
des Musées Nationaux / Art Resources, NY, SO157970 ART154374

crop in June. The winged females fly in search of other *Ficus
carica* trees bearing fruit, in order to lay their eggs. The practice
of hanging branches of the wild fig infested with these insects
facilitates the entire process, known as caprification.

Wasps will enter either common figs or caprifigs, provided
that the fruit is at the right stage. If eggs are deposited in the
caprifig fruit, a new generation of wasps will grow and the
pollen will be wasted. But if the wasp pollenizes the common
fig, then edible fruit will result and no eggs will be laid (the
wasp's ovipositor is too short to place its eggs in the fig's
long-styled female flowers). Note that when the wasp enters
the syconium, it loses it wings, dies, and is absorbed into the
developing fruit.

In short, a fig becomes a mature fruit only after pollination is performed by an insect forcing its way through the terminal pore of the syconium receptacle and losing its wings and life in the process. Although fig trees are not cultivated, their fruit requires the intervention of fig wasps in order to attain maturity. The insects are bred for the purpose of carrying pollen from the caprifig, a wild variety grown with care despite its uselessness in other respects. The symbolism points to a fundamental lesson: self-sterile fig trees yield food on condition that mortals (humans, insects) engage in acts of self-consuming labour and reproduction and acquire the knowledge thereof.

Figs point to the Great Divide between man and woman and between life and death, rifts unknown before the Fall. They stand in direct opposition to the apple, which is often viewed as the fruit of immortality that grew in the Garden of Eden, prior to Adam and Eve eating the apple and committing their first sin. Since they are self-fertile, apple trees can embody the secret of immortality. The notion that "an apple a day keeps the doctor away" still reflects this Edenic connection that lies between the sweet-smelling apple and the good life on earth (Song 2:5, 7:8). By contrast, figs embody the Fall, the self-impotent condition of man and woman who depend on one another to reproduce. They announce a life of uncertain fruition attained through painful travail. Witness the lines delivered immediately after the fig apron scene:

Unto the woman he said, I will greatly multiply thy sorrow and thy conception; in sorrow thou shalt bring forth children; and thy desire shall be to thy husband, and he shall rule over thee. And unto Adam he said, Because thou hast hearkened unto the voice of thy wife, and hast eaten of the tree, of which I commanded thee, saying, Thou shalt not eat of it: cursed is the ground for thy sake; in sorrow shalt thou eat of it all the days of thy life; Thorns also and thistles shall it bring forth to thee; and thou shalt eat the herb of the field; In the sweat of thy face shalt thou eat bread, till thou return unto the ground; for out of it wast thou taken: for dust thou art, and unto dust shalt thou return (Gen. 3.16–19).

Fig cultivation illustrates a fact of the human condition: reproduction feeds upon the exertion of physical labour, economic
(male) and procreational (female). Survival thrives on the pains
of woman giving birth and man working himself to death, just
like the wasp that dies after penetrating and pollinating the fig
syncarp. Given these associations, little imagination is needed
to make sense of the contemptuous fig gesture now known as
the "fico" curse – the thumb thrust between the first two fingers
or under the upper teeth. The gesture is a reminder of the curse
and sufferings of sex and labour.

The fruit of shame separating man from woman and mortals
from immortals provides us with a good example of how language assigns basic dualities to the world we live in. But there
is more to this fruit than a diacritic marker of the divergent
paths that Genesis assigns to Creator and creation and to man
and woman. Fig symbolism is also a good example of the
syncretic activity required to construct images of cleavages in
life and history.

Lines of divergence can be drawn via language as long as
they are situated within common grounds. At the risk of repeating ourselves, oppositional reticles must be located within
broader planes of convergence. Figs can be granted divisive
implications provided they are selected from a larger domain,
in this case, the botanical and the biblical involving other imageries. This is to say that the tribulational implications of the fig
imagery can be underlined in Genesis 3 on condition that they
are situated against other sign impulses of the same category,
those vested in biblical plant imagery. The scriptures deploy a
wide range of plant motifs that occupy diverse positions within
the botanical domain and permit variable connections to a
plurality of themes, sexuality included. Although figs may be
highlighted in the story of Adam and Eve, their meanings and
implications must be understood in relation to other possible
choices made explicit in other scenes. The fig makes sense *in
connection to* the apple, the olive, the oak, and the wormwood,
plants evoking health, peace, idolatry, and calamity, respectively.
A diacritic effort at singling out a sign of separation does not

eradicate larger field connections. However divisive it may be, the fig apron motif evolves within larger semiotic fields.

When language triggers a sign impulse, producing a "meaningful action potential," it does so within a larger field. The field is activated even if it is *not* the focus of attention. As long as this larger reticle remains active, if only implicitly (as opposed to being fully extinguished), the choice sign can prompt cognate symbols going in similar directions. For instance, the fig-apron motif can easily evoke the withering of vines and fig trees, another imagery to signify an act of punishment by God (Ps. 105: 33). While the field remains extant, the choice sign can also retain its ability to distinguish itself from same-field (botanical) motifs going in other directions. The fig apron will thus evoke a movement away from the fruit of knowledge (the apple?) and immortality planted in the Garden of Eden. The figs of Genesis 3 feed into these broader fields of plants of the same or the opposite kind.

But there is another sense in which the fig imagery activates a field of convergence, "bringing things together" despite its main mission, which is to pull things apart (man from woman, Creator from Creation). The fig apron of Genesis 3 triggers a field through sign condensation, a convergence effect that plays a crucial role in semiosis. Condensation consists in the compression of multiple implications in a single imagery. In the context of Genesis, the fig serves to separate mortals from immortals and one sex from the other. Notwithstanding its divisive mission, the power of this symbol lies in its ability to convey both divisions *at once*. Two divisions are packed into one sign. A single tree species answers two questions in a single contextual breath: how life after the Fall demarcates itself from life in Eden, and how one gender distances itself from the other after the curse. Complex issues of life and sex are squeezed into a single-motif terrain.

The plane of convergence entails syncretic reticles of contextualization and condensation. Implications coalesce within signs, and signs evolve within broader grounds wherein differences can play themselves out (as between man and woman, mortals and immortals). Signs consist of fields of implications and sites within fields; using a particular sign means choosing one site and related implications within the larger field. Convergent activity does not stop here, though. Each sign is also a field of "meaningful resting potentials" – a field of connections that may be polarized and remain temporarily impermeable, without impulse transmission. This is a field within which connective choices must be made, activating some and leaving others "at rest," for example, using the fig to signify *either* the Fall *or* the good life enjoyed "under a vine and a fig tree." The fig-field thus acts as a complex surface in its own right, a land packed with alternative connections that are mutually incompatible. Like neural impulses, sign actions can branch out in different directions (but not all of them), depending on what is being communicated.

The biblical fig motif can serve to illustrate this point. We have seen how the fig can act as a sign of the tribulations associated with the downfall of man and woman. But the fig imagery can trigger alternative meanings. It can be chosen to signify states other than a primordial rupture in history. Generally speaking, the scenario known as (1) the Fall can be demarcated from three other states: namely, (2) the good life that used to prevail in Eden; (3) the sinful conduct that man and woman indulged in immediately before the curse; and (4) the sacrificial behaviour that humans must engage in so as to redeem themselves from the Fall.

The good life and the act of sin come before the curse; sacrifice comes after. The fig apron in Genesis 3 takes on the woeful aspects of option 1. This differs from other biblical scenes evoking not the tribulational but rather the joyful (living in a garden of plenty), the sinful (eating the forbidden fruit), or the sacrificial (renouncing fruit of the flesh) moments of life on earth. The fig motif is well suited to expressing the sufferings of man divided from woman and life from death. The point to be made here, however, is that the same motif lends itself to scriptural scenarios other than the Fall. In principle, the fig action potential can be sent in any of the four semantic directions listed above. That is, it can serve to express either sufferings of the Fall, sin as its cause, the Edenic state that preceded it, or the moral remedies thereof. The actual choice to be made depends on the connections to be highlighted in a given text and speech context. Paradoxically, a sign such as the fig is both a location within a larger field and a microcosm of the field itself.

This brings us to three other sets of fig associations that have a direct bearing on the story of Adam and Eve, connections that are not strictly tribulational. Consider signs of the joyful life, the kind that is diametrically opposed to stories of the Fall. Despite the curse it evokes, the ficus is an integral part of the scriptural definition of the blessings of civilization and may even stand for the tree of life planted in the Garden of Eden (as in Jewish tradition). Historically, fig trees abounded in Palestine and Egypt, and the fruit was dried and eaten the year round. It was a source of daily sustenance both fresh and in dry form and was used as a poultice in medicine. Failure of the trees to produce amounted to a tragedy for the common people who lived on the figs. Fig trees grew abundantly, their wood provided durable construction material, and their shade was greatly valued. Most worldly aspirations are thus met by the biblical expression of a man dwelling under his vine and his fig tree, in the comfortable shade of its large leaves, an expression synonymous with peace and security.[6] In the same Edenic spirit, mention should be made of the Shulamite girl, Solomon's fountain of gardens, a woman dressed *in full fig*, hence as a lily-of-the-valley and a showy orchard of pleasant fruit. Her lover's call was said to coincide with fig trees offering green fruit at springtime (Song 2.13, 4.13).

But there is a problem with indices of the good life: they become sinful when enjoyed without restraint. Accordingly, the fig imagery can rot and turn evil, just like human beings. Figs and fig trees, like humans, are not all created equal in the eyes of God. Early figs that appear at springtime are held to be the most beautiful and delicious (Song 2.13, Hos. 9.10). The trees, however, do not always bear fruit of this quality, as confirmed in Matthew (7.16) and Jeremiah (24.1–8). Nor, for that matter,

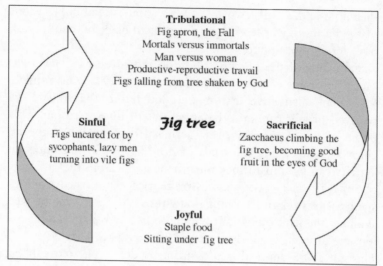

Tribulational
Fig apron, the Fall
Mortals versus immortals
Man versus woman
Productive-reproductive travail
Figs falling from tree shaken by God

Sinful
Figs uncared for by
sycophants, lazy men
turning into vile figs

Fig tree

Sacrificial
Zacchaeus climbing the
fig tree, becoming good
fruit in the eyes of God

Joyful
Staple food
Sitting under fig tree

Variations on fig imagery

do they always bear fruit, especially if they have not received the care of human labour. God can be expected to destroy the vines and the fig trees that feed the lazy. Destruction awaits trees of sin that attract the "sycophant" (a parasite, from Gr. *sykophantes*, literally a "fig shower") who wishes to eat the fruit thereof without the caring of labour.[7]

Figs that feed the lazy are bound to turn into signs of tribulation, a sombre outcome that brings us to back to indices of the Fall. Just as God may castigate a nation for its failure to perform the work of the Lord, so he may curse or cut down a fig tree because of its fruitlessness or the negligence of men turning into "evil figs" (Jer. 24.8). When this happens, the falling of a fig from its tree, or leaf from the vine, serves to indicate the descent of God's wrath on sinful men at autumn. The scene takes place in the days of the final harvest and the sun's fall below the celestial equator (Isa. 34.4). In the words of the Bible (Nah. 3.12–15), "if they [the figs] be shaken, they shall even fall into the mouth of the eater ... the gates of thy land shall be set wide open unto thine enemies ... There shall the fire devour thee; the sword shall cut thee off, it shall eat

thee up like the cankerworm." Other tribulational implications
of the fig motif, those evoking the afflictions of human travail,
have already been explored.

Sufferings of the human condition, however, can be put to
sacrificial usage. This brings us to the last series of fig connections. The distinctive feature of good figs is that they have
received proper care and the attentions of human labour. This
points to the possibility of a sacrificial deployment of the fig
cultivation imagery. The trials of productive and reproductive
activity can be transformed into virtue and lead to the offerings
of abnegation. The edifying lesson that can be learned from fig
symbolism is relatively simple: only those who keep the fig tree
shall eat the fruit thereof, attending to its needs like a shepherd
looking after its flock (Prov. 27.18, Amos 7.14, Luke 13.6–9).
The good life enjoyed while sitting under a fig tree can be
secured only if deserved, hence renounced. Figs must be cared
for and remain unspoiled so that their virtue will be preserved
until they are harvested. If not, fruit of flesh will turn into signs
of retribution, fruits not all that delectable after all.

The story of Zacchaeus as portrayed in miracle plays of the
Middle Ages points to the same moral. Because of its dense
foliage and seminude bark or bare-bark patches which are most
conspicuous in winter, the European sycamore maple (*Acer
pseudo-platanus*) was used in the medieval miracle plays to represent the fig tree, which small-statured Zacchaeus climbed for
a glimpse of the Saviour. Zacchaeus was a wealthy tax collector
who had every opportunity to "sit under a fig tree," enjoying
peace and material security and eating the fruit thereof. Instead,
he climbed the tree, as if to make a gesture of reconciliation
with higher pursuits. He sought to become "good fruit" in the
sight of God. This meant not giving a fig for all the fruit and
blessings of life that men normally pursue, such as the wealth
from which Zacchaeus detached himself, and above which he
finally rose (1 Kings 4.25, Luke 19.2–10). Instead of enjoying
the good life, the small man behaved sacrificially. He behaved
as food that "shall fall into the mouth of the eater" (Nah. 3.12).

In his own way he adopted the humbleness of a mustard seed, which is the only way that man can be granted the power to master the proud mulberry tree (Luke 17.6).

In sum, the fig tree may stand for peace and the blessings of civilization. But we saw that a fig tree can also stand for acts of sinful behaviour, as exemplified by "sycophants" idly sitting in its comfortable shade, like vile and useless figs fallen from the tree and rotting on the ground. When fully explored, this downfall imagery can be converted into a great ordeal: God cursing the fig tree and men alike, making them bare, casting them away, and condemning them to be devoured by their enemies and the sufferings of travail. The Fall is not irreversible, however. If fully assumed, as penance for one's sins, the sufferings of life can be turned into a life of virtue and sacrifice, hence the careful labour needed to secure plentiful fig and the blessings of life on earth. In its own way, the fig loops the entire biblical loop – tying the blessed life to sin, sin to fall, fall to sacrifice, and sacrifice back to the blessings of life on earth.

The fig leaves of Genesis 3 divide at least two things: mortals from immortals, and man from woman. But there is no "pulling apart" without some "bringing together." Through mechanisms of condensation, the tribulational implications of the Fall are packed into a single motif selected from a larger botanical terrain. The plane of convergence weaves itself through the fabric of language in yet another way. It does so by means of multiple choices pressed into a single motif; alternative scenarios converge on the same imagery. In Genesis 3 the fig imagery speaks to digital dualities governing a particular outlook on the human condition. The same fig symbolism, however, can potentially evoke less divisive implications that equally follow from stories of the Fall. Even when used digitally (following a binary system), the fig imagery acts like an analogical field, a terrain where all figurative choices appear in the same narrative equation – the full story of things that come before and after the Fall.

Like hemlocks (are they evergreen trees or poisonous weeds?), fig trees can be given either negative or positive connotations.

All depends on the actual text that deploys the imagery and the multiple meanings readers are entitled to extract from this botanical motif, at least those allowed by convention. But readers are certainly not at liberty to determine the dominant associations of hemlocks in *Evangeline* or figs in Genesis. Longfellow's hemlocks are hooked up to other narrative signs in such ways as to be read primarily as tall excurrent trees of the evergreen pine family, hence signs of convergence in time and space. By contrast, figs in the First Book of Moses are tied to the divergent paths inflicted upon mortals and immortals immediately after man and woman ate the fruit of sin. Adam and Eve covered their shameful nudity with aprons of fig leaves and coats of animal skins and were then cursed with the necessity to labour in sorrow and to till a ground full of thorns and poisonous thistles (Gen. 3.7, 17–21). Yet alternative sign action potentials of the hemlock and the fig are not entirely obliterated. Less apparent connections that serve to divide things otherwise united (the poisonous hemlock), or unite things otherwise divided (Zacchaeus's fig sacrifice), are simply pushed into the background. While they may go off in particular directions at certain points in time, the same sign cells can always use other situations to reticulate elsewhere.

The Corn Boy and the Iguana

Two kinds of sign tissues have been explored in previous reticles. On the one hand, we examined sign weavings suggesting high levels of syncretic assemblage, whether proper name denotations (my signature), signs of condensation (the fig apron), or expressions of mediation (the forest primeval). Although syncretically formed, these assemblages require that the meaningful distance that keeps one sign apart from another should be kept alive. Jacques can be attached to Chevalier and the two names can be assigned to an individual on condition that each proper name signify *something different*. The oneness of a person's proper identity is syncretic, not synthetic. Likewise, the J.C. assemblage cannot be so fused that the name will be confused with the named; one cannot "stand for" the other in the sense of being exactly the same. Signs can be syncretized, provided that distinctions and divisions are fully sustained.

On the other hand, previous analyses also explored signs of rupture and duality generated through diacritic activity. Although designed to work disjunctively, signs of *diakritikos* were shown to activate lines of convergence of their own. The fig apron motif evokes radical divergences in time and space (in and out of Eden), yet it also brings together issues of production and sexuality into a larger story centring on the Creator and his moral creation. It is by virtue of these common grounds that the fig imagery of Genesis 3 can signify dualities inscribed in the human condition and the many trials that followed.

Diacritic processing is never absolute. Signs that have nothing in common cannot connect, not even by way of contrast. What is the difference between a dinosaur and a cup of tea? When pulled out of the blue, such questions are nonsensical and plainly laughable or unanswerable. The syncretic mind is at pains to locate the field of sameness shared by the two signs, a field within which differences can play themselves out.

Are lines of converge essential to all expressions of *diakritikos*? Consider one of the strongest manifestations of dual thinking: a mythical duel between hero and foe. The following material is an illustration of antagonistic imagery taken from present-day Mexican Gulf Nahua mythology (the mythical battle of a dinosaur and a cup of tea has yet to be imagined). It involves the confrontation of an iguana and a deity known as *Sintiopiltsin*, the seed of corn. The myth revolves around the corn child's pilgrimage to the burial ground of his father and his quest for immortality (see Chevalier and Buckles 1995: 274–336).

The idiom spoken by the people of Pajapan corresponds to the "t" dialect of Nahua, as opposed to the "tl" variant spoken by other groups. In the discussion below, words or expressions currently used in Pajapan are both italicized and underlined (e.g., *megat*). By contrast, ancient Nahua terms recorded by Siméon are simply underlined (mecatl). Spanish words appear in italics only. My spelling of classical Nahuatl and Gulf Nahua words follows the conventions adopted by Siméon and García de León respectively.

The myth begins with an old man and his wife discovering two eggs in a milpa, eating one (the female) and preserving the other. A young boy is born from the egg and grows up to become *Sintiopiltsin*, the "venerable son of the corn god." The divinity is also known as *Tamakastsin*, "the little priest," *Itamatiosinti*, the "wise maize god," Homshuk in Soteapan (Blanco Rosas 1992), or San Isidro Labrador in the village of Zaragoza (García de León 1966, 1991: 35). The second scene, the one we shall focus on, portrays the child going to fetch water for the adoptive father who found him in his milpa. At the site of a well the child meets with a few iguanas who make fun of his "ears cut" and tell him where his real father is, namely, in _Tagatauatsaloyan_, "the place where men are dry:"

And there were iguanas (_bagetspalimeh_) there that were making fun (_pinahtiayah_) of the boy. They said "_elote_, _elote_, cut ears (_nagastan-pepel_), your father is over there, in the land where men are dry (_Tagatauatsaloyan_)." They came to inform (_ginotsaya_) the boy. He didn't know (_agimatia_) what they were saying. They were just saying "_elote_, _elote_, cut ears, your father (_motah_) is over there, in the land where men are dry."

The boy eventually uses a lasso to catch one animal by the tail and then decides to let his prey go.[8]

Once again, the scene can be translated into similarities, oppositions, and mediations governing the material at hand, as expressed in the Nahua language.[9] Insights into these operations require that attention should be paid to the language informing the myth. Notwithstanding Lévi-Straussian claims to the contrary, the idiom used to relate a story is a key ingredient of the logical code ruling over the symbolic order. A few remarks concerning the agglutinative features of the Mexican Gulf Nahua dialect are especially important in this regard. The Nahua idiom spoken in southern Veracruz comprises simple and composite words. The former are few in number and can be shortened, extended, duplicated (through syllabic repetition), or compounded to produce new words. Composite nouns, consisting usually of two terms, constitute the majority of words used by Nahua speakers. New meanings are generated through the juxtaposition and agglutination of simple substantives, adjectives, verbs, and adverbs, to which can be added a number of prefixes and suffixes. In addition, root words have meanings that vary from one context to another. Given these features, the language creates no illusion of "things" or proper "identities" (locations, people) that can be denoted univocally, without

The mocking iguana (drawing by Martin Blanchet)

compositional devices. Practically every word is a composition pointing to the relational aspects of things and actions that make up the world as we know it.

At first sight, the corn-iguana antagonism draws lines primarily on the plane of divergence. The story allows conflict to play itself out through the confrontation of plant hero and animal foe. Given their active opposition, we can presume the hero and his mortal enemy to be radically different. But what is it exactly that opposes the animal and the plant deity? Do they have distinct attributes that might fit into a two-column model exhibiting maximum contrast? Could the corn-iguana duel be treated as an expression of dual thinking, with limited effects of convergence and unity if at all?

In reality, a structural emphasis on binary thinking would not do justice to this myth. The conflict that pits the corn boy against the iguana lies not in mere difference. More to the point, the antagonism stems from competing claims to the logic of mediation. The two characters have a lot in common: both strive in their own ways to undo forces of discontinuity and discord affecting life as defined by the Gulf Nahuas. As we are about to see, the encounter between hero and foe speaks to their common aspiration to the blessings of harmony and unity *and competing responses to such hopes*. To use the language of neuropsychology, the corn-iguana battle is not symptomatic of LH thinking; rather, it points to an LH struggling between two ways of soliciting the services of RH syncretic mediation.

The iguana is a powerful mediator. On the spatial level, the creature walks with four legs, it lives near water and mangrove swamps, and it is a good swimmer. Like a fish or a serpent, it has a body covered with scales and a mighty tail to either punish or protect itself from its enemies (García de León 1991: 30). Rumour has it in Pajapan that the reptile has ophidian flesh due to its habit of mating with snakes. The animal also resembles a bird; it lays eggs (thirty to fifty), dwells in trees, and eats fruit, insects, and eggs.[10] In short, the trickster-like iguana or "forest lizard" (*baguetspalin*)[11] has no problem in moving freely between land, water, and sky, thereby mediating the high and the low. What is more, the animal embodies the good life. It is not only good to eat but also a prolific begetter and a voracious eater, a glutton (cuetzpal).

Gifted as it is, the iguana has every reason to make fun of the corn child. The boy is no match for the animal. As a result, he is mocked (*pinahtiayah*) by iguanas while fetching water at the well. The animals make fun of his "cut ears" (*nagastan-pepel*, drooping, hairless)[12] and tell the *elote* boy where his real father is, "in the land where men are dry" (*Tagatauatsaloyan*). An *elote* is maize after three months of growth, beyond the immature *xiloti* stage, with leaves of husk that have begun to dry. Though still in the milk stage and not dry enough to be harvested or to produce seed for future generations, the *elote* grains are already formed and can be eaten on the cob or be ground to produce fresh-maize *tamales* or *tortillas*. This growth stage is normally reached just before the arrival of the heavy

Corn in the field (photograph taken in Pajapan, Veracruz, Mexico, by Daniel Buckles)

rains of September and October brought by tropical storms in the Gulf of Mexico. These storms are followed by the cold, gusty *nortes* blowing from October through March. In order to promote drying and protect *elote* ears against wind and water, the stalks are bent over or "doubled" below the lowest ear once the corn has reached maturity. The upper part of the stalk is usually tied to the lower with the maize leaves. The iguanas seem to be laughing at the sight of the corn-child's "doubled ears."

In a Zoque-Popoluca variant (López Arias 1983), the corn boy identifies himself as *clavito y a la vez dobladito* – nail-like yet doubled. The plant boy is standing up but also bowing down before the mighty winds and rains of the high sea. Corn-eating pigeons and grackles also make fun of his red hair and threaten to eat him. The red-hair attribute assigned to the hero converges again on signs of immaturity. The plant creature feeding on water and light (*tauil*) partakes in the redness (tlauhyo, *tatahuic*) of the morning sun rising at "dawn" (tlauizcalli, light-house), literally "lighting up" while ascending through the "red house" to the east or south-east (tlauhcopa), beyond the sea.[13]

The corn boy has yet to reach full maturity. He is torn between the beginnings of life in water and the requirements of helio-tropic growth. The old man who adopts him faces the opposite problem. As with all men who work the land, the old man experiences thirst while labouring. A dry mouth indicates that someone is "dying of thirst" (amigui) and is in a state of want.[14] Logically, a man who is aging, moving away from life-that-begins-in-water, will suffer from thirst. The corn child's real father suffers a similar fate in that he dwells in _Tagatauat-saloyan_, "the land where men are dry." The term combines the word for "man," _tagat_, with _uatza_, to dry, to become weak or to drain oneself sexually; _tauatzal_ denotes something that has been tanned or dried (_uaktok_). According to García de León (1969: 303–4; 1976: 138), the mythical land in question is of pre-Hispanic origin and is located in the highland Papaloapan valley, west of Pajapan. The site corresponds to _galagui tonati_, "the house where the sun enters," hence the sun aging and disappearing beyond the mountains at the end of the day. The sun's westerly house lies far away from the sea, opposite from _guiça tonati_, which is "where the sun comes out" or "begins."[15]

In short, the young corn child is to his father what the wet lowland is to the dry upland, the east to the west, the morning light to the evening darkness. They are what the reign of life is to the rule of death. In the end, both father and son can be mocked as they lack the ability to reconcile opposite moments in time and locations in space.[16] The opposite can be said of the iguana. The animal rivals the corn god in its ability to counter the afflictions and divisions of life. Given these pow-ers, the _baguetspalin_ can make fun of the young _Sintiopiltsin_. Although born from an egg-like seed and feeding on water and sun, the young plant is doomed to grow with the constant fear (tepinaualiztli)[17] of drowning in water or drying in the sun.

The corn-iguana scene does not illustrate mere dualism – how a manichean code carves up reality into component parts that will not let themselves be reconciled. The imagery shows rather how language can propose alternative ways of attenuating the contradictions of its own making. Apparently some mediators are better at doing this than others. Syncretic unity is achieved with uneven success, depending on the strategy adopted and the hero elected to carry the torch. To put it differently, dualities are subject to variations in levels of mediation; while some are closer to admissions of discord, others point to effects of harmony verging on perfect unity. Syncretic connectivity is a matter of amplitude.

A prolific and gluttonous iguana moving between water, earth, and sky seems to have all the mediatory powers it takes to triumph over the corn boy. But the story does not end here. The animal is captured and scolded by the corn boy. Why is this so? Could it be that great weakness lies in the lizard's strength? As a gluttonous creature and a corn-eating parasite, the animal lacks what is needed to reconcile the good life with the requirements of growth, aging, and reproduction. Unlike the corn god, it cannot address the paradox of cycles of life and death on earth; it simply dies off, without giving higher meaning to death. Accordingly, Gulf Nahua mythology assigns basic limitations to what the iguana can do to resolve problems of the human condition. In exchange the corn hero (doubling itself and drying at autumn in order to feed humans who will reproduce the plant) offers a "higher" strategy to secure the blessings of human and plant life, a strategy that speaks to the teachings of asceticism and the basic requirements of survival through corn cultivation.

In *The 3-D Mind 3*, we return to this native formulation of sacrificial morality, ascetic teachings without the Judeo-Christian depreciation of nature. For the moment, suffice it to say that the Nahua battle between two forms of mediation, the hedonistic and the ascetic, is skewed from the start. By downplaying distances in time and space, the first strategy appeals to a syncretic and holistic predilection for ready-made signs of unity and harmony. The second strategy, however, implies a more complex and durable integration of syncretic and diacritic imageries, higher-level communications achieved through paradoxical linkages. Through lessons of the Corn God, sacrificial reasoning permits exchanges between contraries, a far cry from signs of their final dissolution vested in the vain iguana.

This completes our illustration of how language interweaves lines of convergence and divergence, in ways that are responsive to context. Sign action potentials generate variegated patterns of similarities and differences that lend themselves to uneven levels of mediation. While the name Jaques M. Chevalier and Longfellow's forest primeval imagery constitute sign reticles mapped predominantly on to the plane of convergence, the corn-iguana battle scene and the fig-apron motif map out divergent paths not amenable to immediate arbitration (reconciling enemies, or life in and out of Eden). These contrasts notwithstanding, one "signaptic" mode can hardly prevail over the other without contralateral supplementation. Bilateral sign action is a requirement of semiosis.

PHILOSOPHICAL LINES

A Theoreticle Approach

Having dealt with brain laterality issues and how lessons of neuropsychology can be extended to products of language and symbolling, I now wish to address the question of how studies in "neurosemiotics" can be linked up with broader philosophical considerations. My answer to this query lies in what I am tempted to call a "theoreticle" perspective, a fugitive inscription that refuses full presence and representation in speech, as with Derrida's *différance*.

My outline of a "theoreticle" approach brings together various contributions that stress the processual nature of sign reticulation. Although limited in their actual use, terms such as "process" and "reticle" can address the manifold functions of semiosis: that is, the active and interactive (below), the divisive and "chaosmic" (reticle 12), the connective and configurative (reticle 13) aspects of sign activity. As we are about to see, these multiple functions suggest that sign processes are methods of doing things, courses of action performed on both planes of convergence and divergence, meaningful actions evolving "in the middleness" of other communicative actions. An argument will be made for a "mathematical" understanding of sign middleness, an interpretive strategy that applies measures of (RH) "integral" and (LH) "differential" calculus to sign quantities and pragmatics of the phenomenal world.

A "theoreticle" philosophy of this sort precludes metaphysical accounts of signs viewed as links between ghostly things and thoughts in chronic need of denotation and "representation."

Semiosis is not an instru-mental language that self-conscious, sign-making subjects will use to signify objects and ideas as they see fit. The argument outlined below also eschews temptations to fit the rhizomatic variegations and multiplicities of sign prag-matics into neat models of dualistic reasoning and related mea-sures of logical or dialectical mediation. As in Deleuzian theory, reticular activity can be shown to differ radically from arbores-cent thinking and the order of divarication (logical forking or branching apart).

Semiosis is neither immaterial nor metaphysical. Far from being a kindred "spirit of the mind," the sign process is a ner-vous brain-and-body activity involving massive quantities of electrical and chemical events. Activities ranging from verbal utterances and writing to body language and visual processing require the deployment of billions of action potentials. Although amazingly microscopic, these synaptic actions add up and develop into complex processes of organic and social behaviour. This is to say that brains at work do not generate a passive representation or mirror reflection of the world. Nor are they in the business of manufacturing ethereal concepts and ideas depicting phenomena perceived by the senses. More realistically, sign processes entail *courses of action* or *methods of doing* things that are physical and informational all at once. Thus there is absolutely nothing ethereal about speaking or even "think-ing." The same can be said of all products of brain processing, whether they consist in listening, speaking, writing, counting, eating, or cooking. In the words of Baudrillard (1990: 6), signs woven into phenomenal appearances are "simply the sovereign unfolding of the body and movement."

Distinctions between mind and body are called in question. Variations on this dualism are many. They include the divisions of subject and object, thought and action, conception and per-ception, idea and behaviour, the abstract and the concrete, the true and the real. Echoes of these Cartesian mind/body binaries can be heard in stories of consciousness battling against libido. They can also be found in the privacy of one's home – in the differences we establish between owning subjects and the objects they privately own (including "one's home"). To these familiar distinctions can be added the dual genealogy of affinity (subjective, chosen) and consanguinity (objective, ascribed), principles of kinship embedded in the modern lifeworld. When viewed sociologically, dualism *à la* Descartes tends to assimilate all sign processes to some "sort of cultural surf frothing on the beachhead of the economy," surf frothing on the firm ground of physicality and materiality (Baudrillard 1981: 144). In bourgeois and Marxist thought alike, culture ends up being embalmed and mummified into some pseudo-transcendental consciousness. The entity then turns into a collective mind, a shared spirit either to be exalted as the vehicle of social value and morality or to be denounced as ideology and false consciousness misrepresenting the real. The debate brings us back to the right and the left, as it were.

But there is nothing new here. Suspicion about the truth value of mind/body dualities is now so widespread as to be common currency. In the end these exercises in doubt may be wasted. After all, why bother to charge the metaphysical mind with a crime no force can conceivably commit: misrepresenting a world that won't let itself be represented in the first place? Would it not be more appropriate to simply recognize the mind/body divide as a plane of divergence in its own right, with a history of methods of doing and courses of action of its own? Instead of trying to sap its truth foundations, should we not explore practical mediations of the mind/body difference – how the difference is embedded and handled in institutions and events of western history?

This is what Baudrillard (1981: 144–6) proposes. In his view western culture is committed to the production of economic and symbolic values that both divide and connect the cultural and the natural, the subjective and the objective. The resulting lifeworld, however, presupposes a bifurcation of values invested in *commodities and signs*. The commodity form prevalent in market economies is a twofold assemblage. On the one hand, it contains a use-value "naturally" deemed to satisfy needs of the body. On the other hand, when commoditized, concrete use-values embody something which is not strictly physical or natural. Use-values acquire a socially determined exchange-value, an abstract exchangeability measured through prices that are inherently commensurable. Both aspects of economic value come together in activities of commodity production and consumption ruled by capital.

A similar dualism applies to signs manufactured on the cultural plane. The economic bifurcation of use and equivalence is paralleled by a logic of sign conventions divided into literal denotations and subjective connotations. These constitute the use-values and exchange-values of language, respectively. Just as goods and services deconstruct into measures of usability and exchangeability, so too words bifurcate into concrete reference (object denotation) and abstract signification (conceptual meaning).

These divisive operations generate linguistic and economic processes requiring a concrete and natural grounding of "mental" activity carried out through manifest sign events. Like commodities, signifiers appear to be caught in the middle of "concrete things" and "abstract thoughts." While they are as tangible as sounds or as images can be, they are founded in ideas and the things or phenomena they represent. Signs ask to be processed accordingly, in conformity with the two-sided rule of logic and the senses. Similarly, commodity prices are grounded in the real use-values they stand for and are managed in accordance with the laws of material supply and demand. In both cases the concrete serves as a stepping stone for the abstract, and the abstract as a means to master the concrete. True to form, society divides itself up into subjects who engage in conceptual activity (managers, intellectuals) and those who do the actual work (labourers).

The double aspect of the commodity (UV/EV) in fact conceals a formal homogeneity in which use value, regulated by the system of exchange value, confers on the latter its "naturalist" guarantee. And the double face of the sign (Sr/Sd [signifier/signified], generalizable into Sr/Sd – Rft [referent]) obscures a formal homogeneity in which Sd and Rft (administered by the same logical form, which is none other than that

of the Sr), serve together as the reference-alibi – precisely the guarantee of "substance" for the Sr (Baudrillard 1981: 155–6).

Baudrillard's claim is that the natural use-value fiction masks
the decisive role of the exchange-value principle that commands
the general commodity form. Likewise, the signified (concept)
and the referent (object) play the role of use-value within the
metaphysics of representation; the usefulness of signifiers resides
in the thoughts and things they are designed to represent. The
implication of Baudrillard's theory is that theories of language
and political economy that fail to situate these assumptions in
their proper historical and cultural context are in danger of
internalizing and reinforcing premises of capitalism and metaphysics of the mind. Critiques of culture and ideology, be they
couched in the language of liberal humanism, Marxism, radical
feminism, or identity politics, may also end up reproducing
these assumptions somewhat uncritically. Critical theory that
seeks to challenge the foundations of western culture must take
care not to judge signs – be they signs of humanity, gender, class
relations, or ethnic identity – on the basis of their adequate
representation of the referential real.
  In reality, distances constructed between signifiers/exchange-
values and what they actually "represent" or "stand for" are
modes of doings things that take on a reality of their own.
More precisely, they are constitutive of sign and material production in capitalist societies. Actions cast in a "representational" mould are thus worthy of being explored at full length,
as opposed to being simply denounced. At the same time they
should not be taken at face value, spreading them around the
world and extending them to all periods of history. However
"real" these methods of doing things may be, they are not
"naturally given." Signs of representational activity may be
second nature to some societies, but history could have managed and could eventually do without them. This is to say that
studies of western metaphysics and the institutions they generate must distance themselves from their own subject matter.
After all, capitalism understood through its own matter/mind

metaphysics will yield little knowledge. No great insight into
the workings of capital is gained by espousing the bourgeois
discourse of rational transactions between objective scarcity
and subjective ends. The same can be said of Marxist views
that pit productive forces and relations against their mental
(mis)representations. They too echo their subject matter as
opposed to pronouncing something new. Both perspectives do
"as if the commodity and the system of material production
'signified' nothing'" (Baudrillard 1981: 146). They ignore the
fact that signs inform all operations of value-attribution and
pervade all moments of material activity, from production to
consumption, and all intervening acts of exchange.

Similar comments apply to the logic of sign representation,
a mode of doing things endowed with its own coordinates in
time and space. Consider practices of literacy and literality
premised on distinctions and one-to-one correspondences
between:

- discrete Srs inscribed in language, be they oral or written (the
  signifier "d-o-g");
- specific Sds, be they mental (the *signified* concept of "dog")
  or oral (the verbal Sr *signified* by the phonetic inscription
  "d-o-g"); and
- particular Rfts embedded in the phenomenal world (the animal
  referent, the one that does the actual barking and biting).

Signifiers directly mapped onto fragments of the phenomenal
world are part of a western sign process that has its own history,
with methods of sign representation centred on practices of use-
value literality and literacy. This representational process treats
denotation as the first among meanings. Barthes's (1970) critique is still relevant here. His argument is that denotation is
no more than the last of connotations, the one that seems to
impose itself upon users of language. Literal meaning is thus
the most subtle moment of signification, the mythical moment
when language struggles to revert to the order of nature constructed in a western perspective. This is the objective order in

relation to which everything else is pure literature or mere ambiguity and imprecision afflicting the subject *qua* subject (ibid.: 157–9).

Representational metaphysics presupposes a distinction between object and concept, each identical to itself and to nothing else. In the end the distinction is merely an invitation, a pretext to establish correspondences and analogical ties between object and concept, to be judged and mediated by the thinking subject and the tools of language consisting of sounds and letters to match. In this perspective the sign operates essentially as a middle point linking an object and a subject's concept.

The argument presented in previous analyses is radically different: the middleness of sign activity lies elsewhere, in the capacity for one sign action to affect and be affected by another. As already explained, signs involve the application of uneven movement, force, and affect on to planes of divergence and convergence, with distributions that can vary *ad infinitum*. This is to say that sign activity never occurs at the level of simple relations, be they well-structured binaries (e.g., thought versus thing) or rigid correlations between single elements or things (the word "dog" to represent the real dog, the one that exists without quotation marks). To use Deleuzian language, sign processes maintain rather a constant capacity to proliferate and multiply connections adapted to varying situations. They constitute "affects" and "intensities" occurring in the middle of open-ended, interconnected plateaus. Sign affects are essentially nomadic, travelling like restless and troublesome demons leaping over limits and operating in the intervals of lawful domains. Like cells (Rosenzweig et al. 1999: 160), signs are prone to migrate and are subject to massive movements aimed at establishing new populations. Their wanderings thus generate errant, delirious, and orgiastic distributions, as opposed to the organic and hierarchical distributions of fixed analogical thinking. "Difference thus appears as the orgiastic representation of determination and no longer as its organic representation" (Deleuze 1994: 43).[18] Sign nomadism contradicts all matrices operating as fixed equational structures. It is a constant challenge to the clear legibility and false transparency of the sign, undermining the use-value of literality and the exchange-value of word representation alike (Baudrillard 1981: 150).

"Cells sort themselves out and take on the fate that is appropriate in the context of what neigboring cells are doing" (Rosenzweig et al. 1999: 161). Signs do the same thing; they act on and react to other signs. Every sign affect is a nervous response to other sign affects. Words respond to other words, verbal utterances to signs of the body, body language to scenes from a film, movements of the eyes to alterations in tone, vocal sounds to ceremonial gestures, ritual performances to political events, social movements to new economic circumstances, and so on. All such responses take the form of actions and events occurring in sequence, as in A leads to B which leads to C. But the causal chain is also transformational. It causes things to actually change, disassembling and reassembling them into other things, just like cells that are subject to synapse rearrangements (ibid.: 160). Signs have a lot in common with sensory transducers that convert energy from one form to another (ibid.: 192). They permit edible stuff found in the raw to be converted into cooked food, in accordance with rules of culinary transformation (Lévi-Strauss 1987: 40). Raw materials are turned into commodities serving the logic of capital; support from capital into parliamentary authority; contractual documents into access to land; marriage vows into legal rights and obligations; images of battling spirits into lessons of sacrifice; and so on. Whether proceeding through causal sequences or reassemblages of the parts, sign activity never escapes the middleness of sign pragmatics and semiotic processing. *Transduction* is a key principle of semiosis.

Being in the middle of practically everything, semiosis requires a "science of the sensible," an expression implying a "superior empiricism" that does away with all formulations of the transcendental subject (Deleuze 1994: 56–7, 277–8). Methods and practices of sign-representation must therefore be challenged if we are to do justice to the physicality of movements of the mind. Signs are not passive expressions of external objects or concepts in need of representation. More realistically, they are active events that pervade all aspects of social reality. Given their lively disposition, signs cannot signify without "acting," they cannot "act" without "acting on," and they cannot "act on" without "reacting to." Words, movement, and nervous activity respond to a wide range of actions and provoke responses of their own.

Signs do not originate from primitive events. They do not dissipate into climactic outcomes and related finalities. Nor can they be ossified into logical rules and static structures.[19] Sign actions are rather like people who are "always in the middle of some business, where nothing may be designated as its origin" (Deleuze and Parnet 1987: 111). They are like myths that vary so much that they can never be traced down to some original beginning (Lévi-Strauss 1963a: 217). They are forces in motion that can never be pinned down to static systems or geared to some final destination. As with synapses, sign connections are shaped by what Nancy (1993: 2, 26ff.) calls "the 'in the midst of taking place' that has neither beginning nor end," a protracted birth-like process that destabilizes fixed identities or illusions thereof and makes them "tremble." All semiotic events take place within courses of action that are permanently "underway." The sign process is an intensity or flux subject to the wheelings of becoming and eternal return, a state of compelling re-petition or *différance* that ignores all grand illusions of full arrest.

Pigeons, Doves, and Ghosts

A sign event is always "in the middle" in the sense of acting on and reacting to many other things. But it is "in the middle" in another sense: a movement or force that draws lines between things, dividing A from B and C, or A from not A. Middle spaces are zones of activity, yet they are also sites of distance and difference. But how should the middleness of signs and the differences they deploy be conceived? Familiar ways of answering the question include the analytical (pigeonholing), the metaphysical (ghost-chasing), and the dialectical (dove-flying).

ANALYTIC PIGEONHOLING

The first answer to the question of difference lies in analytic logic – looking for relations of likeness and distinctiveness and classifying things accordingly. As with concepts and things, signs pigeonholed into analytic slots exist by themselves such that they can be compared, likened, and contrasted. White is the opposite of black; p and b are distinct bilabial consonants; seconds are portions of minutes; the Beast is foe to the Lamb slain. The problem with this approach is that signs are not static positions but rather processes of active differentiation. This is true not only in the realm of language but also in the social domain. Differences in society are not effects of concepts and objects neatly classified into discrete categories and fixed taxonomies, mental constructions removed from the web of social pragmatics (Derrida 1981a: 27). Social life is rather a process that generates meaningful and physical distances between one group or class and another. Processes of distancing and inter-spacing can be applied to an infinite number of relations such as between the masculine and the feminine, the old and the young, gods and humans, owners of capital and wage-labourers, a civil government and a body of citizens, one set of names or species (given names, proper names, *Canis canis*) and another (family names, common names, *Canis lupus*), and so on.

The divisions thus constructed are deployed not so much between things or elements as between other divisions. Sign activity generates spaces between interspaces. The distance that lies between one language and another thus stems from differ-ences in methods of generating and ordering differences of the grammatical, phonetic, or semantic sort (for example, while French genders all nouns, English neuters them). Similar remarks apply to social institutions. Capitalism does not distinguish itself by being an exchange-value economy as opposed to other modes of production featuring a use-value rationality or vari-ation thereof. Rather, capitalism differentiates itself from other economic systems by instituting its own set of differences. When compared to feudal arrangements, the process of capital accumulation constitutes a different assemblage of productive forces and property relations. Feudalism and capitalism artic-ulate material and social differences differently; likewise with polity and family across history. Societies diverge in how they organize their respective divisions and territorialities – inter-spaces between leaders and followers, men and women, the old and the young, one lineage or territory and another.

METAPHYSICAL GHOST-CHASING

The second way to portray the middleness of sign actions is by locating them somewhere between concepts and objects and ranking them on the basis of their relative closeness to things and thoughts. Truth-value is the end goal of this exercise in metaphysical mediation; signs in search of truth chase after ghostly things and thoughts that may exist without ever being seen. The game follows a relatively simple rule: closeness wins over distance. Similarity triumphs over difference, convergence over divergence. The more present signs are to presences in the mind or the world, the more truthful they are. Words spoken in the immediate presence of things and thoughts are favoured in this contest, especially when compared to writing, which proceeds at a greater distance.

Derrida's critique of the phonocentric version of metaphysics is insightful in this regard. Derrida shows how metaphysics of Aristotelian inspiration treats the phonic-verbal system as the privileged site for expressions of presemiotic knowledge, putting upstream thoughts, intuitions, and experiences into half-stream sounds, so to speak. By contrast, writing is a derivative sign system consisting of inscriptions deemed to evolve downstream from the "voice" of conceptual and sensorial consciousness (Derrida 1982: 75, 88). In the words of Saussure, "language and writing are two distinct systems of signs; the second exists for the sole purpose of representing the first" (1966: 23). The speech code comes first logically and chronologically, to the point that writing may obscure natural language, acting as a disguise or even a parasite (Saussure 1966: 25, 30; Jakobson and Halle 1956: 16–17).

To counter the lure of metaphysics, Derrida claims that every signified is in the position of a signifier. Signs speak to other signs. As Peirce and Jakobson argue, meaning points to the mutual translatability of signs, using common metalingual operations ("do you understand what I meant to say?") to interpret signs by converting them into "other, in some respects homogeneous, signs of the same language" (Jakobson 1985: 120; cf. 117–18). This implies that signifiers are under no obligation to pass as substitutes of the signified, be they words standing for thoughts and objects, or "letters" standing for words. The signified is never to be found outside the expressive signifier courting its presence, as in Husserlian phenomenology (Derrida 1981a: 18–23, 31–2). Again, things and thoughts are a lure.

Derrida adds that signs speak to other signs on condition that some distance be preserved and nourished. Inscriptions of writing derive meaning from their differential linkages to other inscriptions. Likewise, words make sense in relation to other words. Signification thrives on formal plays of differences interwoven into texts or text-like fabrics, without any element being so simple and self-sufficient as to refer to nothing else but itself. Derridean grammatology thus pays attention to the rule of *différance*, the prolific spacing by means of which elements interact with one another. The approach precludes elements that are identical to themselves. There are no elements that possess inherent attributes, properties that may or may not be shared with other positive terms and that produce commonalties or contrasts to be discovered through analogy and comparative analysis. In short, what Saussure says of language applies to all semiotic processes. In semiosis there are only differences without positive terms. The idea or phonic substance that a sign contains matters far less than all those signs that surround each and every sign (Derrida 1973: 140–1; 1981a: 25–7).

Sign actions are neither elements nor positions within systems. Rather, they are vectors wired to other vectors, just like a tapestry "produced by the visual oppositions of threads of different colors" (Saussure 1966: 33). As Jakobson (1985: 139) puts it, "we must consistently discuss the problems of language with regard to other problems of signs, such as gestures, graphics, music, etc., and their interrelations." By implication, the sign process is not a function of the speaking subject mentally hovering above the body of language. Instead of being the one that "makes a difference," the subject is constituted by fields of differences. Far from generating a language of differences, the subject is a product of *différance* (Derrida 1973: 82; 1981a: 28–9). This is not to say that language "is the social product deposited in the brain of each individual" (Saussure 1966: 23). Actually, language (viewed broadly as sign activity) is the brain in action, semiosis at work both individually and culturally.

Derrida's attack against metaphysics is devastating and self-defeating at the same time. Notwithstanding its many critics, metaphysics should not be accused of being a "misrepresentation" of what thought and language are all about. The accusation would be a blessing in disguise; although negatively formulated, a "failure to represent" confirms the end goal of knowing the real truth about the mind and signs thereof. More to the point, the discourse of metaphysics is a performance in its own right, a lifeworld revolving around tangible fabrications of concepts and objects whose fate it is to be transformed into appearances of representation first in speech and then in writing. Through immediate thinking and living speech, however, concepts and objects are allowed to enjoy a "relative autonomy." They can impose their presence upon the subject, without visible traces of sign activity. They can assert themselves outside the chain of signification, as in Husserl's moments of solitary mental life (cf. Derrida 1973: 48). This is a necessary condition for their translatability into words, their closest representatives, and letters, their distant postal-like substitutes. The presumption here is that objects exist out there in the real world, in a state of absolute self-presence. If the assumption ends up being challenged (do objects really exist?), the self-presence thesis could still be recuperated through the notion of "real phenomena" and thoughts intuited by the mind. Both are designed to be experienced in their full immediacy, without sign intermediation.

In the self-presence of sensation and consciousness occasionally "expressed" in living speech (with writing serving only as a distant proxy), Derrida sees nothing but a phonocentric illusion or transcendental lure (Derrida 1981a: 5, 8–14, 21–6, 28–9, 33). The lure in question, however, is more powerful and worthy of attention than a mere error of thought. As already suggested, metaphysics is a language evolving on its own stage, a plot that sets up particular acts of *diakritikos*. The action features a signifying process that institutes differences between the inscriptive *gramma* and the spoken words they stand for, and also between words and the things and thoughts they represent. Signs, concepts, and objects are ultimately differentiated from the Sign-Maker, a ghostly role formerly played by God and now by *l'esprit* dwelling in everyone's brain or mind. To this metaphysical script can be added cognate divisions between the intelligible and the sensible, thought and matter, culture and nature.

These are the key interspaces prescribed in the theatre of metaphysics, a sign performance that negates all purely worldly platforms. Although concerned with representation and presence, metaphysics generates the distances and absences required of any language. Logocentric plots thus revolve around signs of non-signs (things, ideas) – signs acting out in a world of differences between matter and mind. The resulting performances are successful as long as non-signs surpass and contradict themselves through a massive deployment of metaphysical props, tricks to "express" or signify the rule of nonexpressivity – the rule of concepts and objects existing in themselves, with or without representation in language. In the end metaphysics is like any other language: it too may be performative and generates imaginary pragmatics of its own.

DIALECTICAL DOVE-FLYING

The position taken above may be read as an invitation to dialectical thinking, a perspective that emphasizes differentiation (obtained through opposition and contradiction) and reciprocal interchange – signs acting like doves flying between upper-world thoughts and lower-world things. But readers should bear in mind that dialectical mediations between subject and object are deeply committed to the polarity they wish to arbitrate. The dual matter/mind edifice will not be shaken by wishful discussions of the dialectical cement that holds the entire structure together. And there is another aspect of dialectical reasoning that is even more problematic: its tendency to fit multiplicities into dualities. We have seen that the sign process entails a nervous production of gaps and crevices spreading themselves out on multiple levels of the phenomenal world. The complexity of this divisive process is of such scope and magnitude that it cannot be reduced to the strictures of binomial mathematics. Like the brain itself, semiosis is a poor candidate for models of binary logic or classificatory thinking, be they couched in the language of structuralism, psychoanalysis, cognitive science, Chomskian linguistics, or Hegelian dialectics (see Deleuze and Guattari 1987: 5, 14, 52; Guattari 1995: 72; Derrida 1981b: 25).

We must concede that "contagious dualism" is an integral part of the operations of language, a bipolar activity that may reach hegemonic proportions. The recursive effects of "dichotomania" represent nonetheless the simplest possible admixture of diacritic and syncretic activity. They consist in mapping a host of differences onto a central opposition or antagonism, treating it as a two-sided terrain upon which all other gaps and fissures can be neatly aligned. Efforts are made to elevate some Great Divide to the rank of a major axis or driving force acting behind all other splits and crevices in language and society. Echoes of this can be found in the role assigned to capital and labour in Marxism, the Berlin Wall that separated communism from the self-proclaimed "free world," the pure and the impure in Dumont's *Homo Hierarchicus*, the battle of body and soul in Christian theology, one gender battling against another in radical feminism, the formation of clans or lineages in dual moiety societies (Lévi-Strauss 1969: 69), and, last but not least, the rivalry of Pepsi and Coca-Cola in American ads. The gathering of all divisions in one central rift can generate a Manichean perspective on reality. But it can also invite a revolutionary struggle to mend a world otherwise rife with conflict. Alternatively, it can invite a fury of middle-of-the-road activities sustained by principal and subaltern arbitrators – say, middle classes and the welfare state mitigating class struggle in advanced capitalism, or animal symbols reducing divisions between culture and nature in totemic societies (Lévi-Strauss 1963a: 215f.; 1963b: 89). The tendency for all splits to converge on a leading categorization and mediation system implies that lines of divergence cannot fully disperse, moving away from and squarely outside the Great Divide and remedies thereof. One Great Cause (say, dialectical materialism) subsumes all other battles (say, religious struggles). It also means that the hegemonic grid can never go astray, leaving its course of action and taking an unfamiliar route leading to some exotic semiosis. Contagious dualism imposes *maximum constraint on lines of dispersal and shifts in perspective*. While a perspective (RH) in its own right, dualism (LH) puts a ban on signs of renegade action and deviating assemblages. Tropical jungles are turned into French gardens.

Compulsive dualism entails a minimal encounter between planes of convergence and divergence. Semiotic binarism and related works of dialectical mediation are governed by the logic of divarication. This is the process whereby things are neatly developed and divided into branches that are fed by the main stem. Though often a powerful force in social history, divarication cannot absorb all moments and sites of sign activity. Semiosis inevitably entails a dispersal of affects and meanings involving wide-open networks, nomadic forces, and movements eluding the false multiplicities of classificatory logic (cf. Deleuze and Guattari 1987: xiii, 21).

As Deleuze (1994) points out, things that "differ" do not necessarily fit into the neatly defined positions of logic and the social order. Not all signs can be massaged into relations of inner-class opposition and higher-class resemblance (e.g., dogs and cats may be different, but they're all domestic animals). The rule of difference is not reducible to principles of organic representation, which include:

- identity in the concept (if a dog, then not a non-dog);
- opposition in the predicate (if a dog that barks, then not a cat that meows);
- analogy in judgment (if a dog, then perhaps a model of companionship and friendship, unlike the cat); and
- resemblance in perception (if both walk on four legs and live in people's houses…).

Signs of diversity – the decentred, the divergent, the disparate – evade these organic principles. They also go beyond identities of representation, the Hegelian negation of negation, and the Aristotelian notion of difference based on the opposition of species within genus.[20] Sign-processing presupposes rather "a swarm of differences, a pluralism of free, wild or untamed differences, a properly differential and original space and time; all of which persist alongside the simplifications of limitation and opposition. A more profound real element must be defined in order for oppositions of forces or limitations of forms to be drawn, one which is determined as an abstract and potential multiplicity. Oppositions are roughly cut from a delicate milieu of overlapping perspectives, of communicating distances, divergences and disparities, of heterogeneous potentials and intensities ... There is a false profundity in conflict, but underneath conflict, the space of the play of differences" (Deleuze 1994: 50f.).

Divisiveness and disparateness are inherent properties of semiosis, which means that "chaosmosis" is the rule. The dominion of "chaosmos" points to the heterogeneity and fractality of sign actions, to be explored through the tools of "schizoanalysis." These terms evoke chaoid variables mapped along the coordinates of productions orchestrated but never unified by the brain (Guattari 1995: 72, 75–6; Deleuze and Guattari 1994: 204, 208).

Signs are polymorphous perverts. Given their wanderings, they will not let themselves be reasoned into simple axioms and principles. They cannot be harnessed to laws that work mechanically and with uniformity. Nor are they conducive to dualistic and dialectical machinations – driven by pivotal contradictions and antagonisms. In lieu of emphasizing order in language and society, students of sign pragmatics should stress the malleability of social "mappings" or "cartography," and hence the vagueness and indeterminacy of a living "chaosmos."[22] What Deleuze and Guattari say of chaos in the brain applies to sign activity. Every sign action manifests "an uncertain and hazardous characteristic, not only in electrical synapses, which show a statistical chaos, but in chemical synapses, which refer to a deterministic chaos. There are not so much cerebral centers as points, concentrated in one area and disseminated in another, and 'oscillators,' oscillating molecules that pass from one point to another." Given these insights, "arborized paradigms" should give way to "rhizomatic figures, acentered systems, networks of finite automatons, chaoid states. No doubt this chaos is hidden by the reinforcement of opinion generating facilitating paths, through the action of habits or models of recognition; but it will become much more noticeable if, on the contrary, we consider creative processes and the bifurcations they imply" (Deleuze and Guattari 1994: 216).

When transposed to social life, the rule of chaosmos is so pervasive that the explanatory value of ideal-types and taxonomies can be considered suspect from the start. Studies of capital and state institutions provide good examples of this. If sensitive to history, studies are bound to show enormous variations and contingencies in the ways that private business (property relations, labour processes) and government affairs (party formation, political institutions, etc.) are carried out (cf. Chevalier and Buckles 1995: 337–40). These variations and adaptations are an integral part of what capitalism and state regimes mean in history. Similar comments apply to the pliable applications of kinship systems (gender, marriage, sexuality, and descent) and the playful expressions of rituals and mythology. They too lend themselves to all sorts of variations and disparities that defy the linear formulations of structure and logic. The indeterminacy and variability of social artifacts preclude ideal-typical characterizations that will box history and culture into their simplest expressions.

In short, the middleness and transitive operations of sign activity contradict all metaphysical, analytical, and dialectical accounts of semiosis. But they also point to the connective properties of sign processing, to which we now turn.

A Jungle in Versailles

Those who get lost in jungles are people who never dwell in them. Although synonymous with entanglements bordering on chaos and confusion, tropical forests are not without landmarks and configurations of water and land. These might be major and secondary affluents, up-river and down-river locations, areas nearer the mountains or the sea, villages and settlements, waterfalls and lakes, paths and trails through the forest, farms and horticultural plots where culture and nature meet. Thus rumours of chaos in the jungle are grossly exaggerated.

Likewise with neural labyrinths and forests of symbols. Signs and synapses are never so "chaosmotic" as to form absolute voids, holes filled with erratic contradictions and negativity, without affirmation and meaning (Deleuze 1994: 52–5, 267f.). However entangled they may be, synaptic clefts are communicational interspaces that permit neurons and chemicals to interact in patterns that feed into broader processes. The same can be said of sign impulses. They establish connections between sign vectors, weaving threads and lines between relations. Semiosis is formed through (and not prior to) the process of "signaptogenesis," from synaptogenesis, the establishment of connections through the growth of axons and dendrites (Rosenzweig et al. 1999: 160). Each sign is the product of reticular activity – sign cells networking through dense fabrics of living pathways forming the "internal linguistic organism" (Saussure 1966: 22). Far from constituting insuperable distances ruled by chaotic spaces, sign actions are lines and communicational events bent on reticulating and concatenating. "There are, as it were, infinite verbs, lines of becoming, lines which shoot between domains and leap from one domain to another, interregnums" (Deleuze and Parnet 1987: 68). Like a patchwork or Harlequin's jacket, sign confederations are "made up of solid parts and voids, blocs and ruptures, attractions and divisions, nuances and bluntnesses, conjunctions and separations, alternations and interweavings, additions which never reach a total and subtractions whose remainder is never fixed" (Deleuze and Parnet 1987: 55).

Signs do not come together via the free association of discrete entities or relations that may or may not assemble. Instead they come together through a compulsion to confederate. Sign actions derive their existence from broader reticular activity and related means of patterning. However intricate it may be, "signaptic" networking introduces order into the chaos of sense data. The sense of congregation thus projected feeds directly into every perception and aggregation of similarities and differences. As Merleau-Ponty writes, it is "because we perceive a grouping as a thing that the analytical attitude can discern likeness or proximities. This does not mean simply that without any perception of the whole we would not think of *noticing* the resemblance or the contiguity of its elements, but literally that they would not be part of the same world and would not exist at all" (Merleau-Ponty 1962: 16). The brain can recognize the details of a grouping provided that it perceives the grouping as a whole.

To use an older terminology, there is more to the assemblage of an object, a scene, or a text than the mere sum of its component parts. This is true of sensory perception in that the contiguity and resemblance of associated stimuli cannot be recognized prior to the constitution of the whole. Things can be associated only if perceived to belong to the same order or field. The rule of confederation is also true of verbal utterances and semiotic activity. A word or image (e.g., the fig imagery in Genesis) that prompts a reply in the form of another word or image (e.g., God cursing Adam and Eve) does not act like a mechanical cause or stimulus producing an external effect or response. A sign event is rather an opportunity to further explore a field already triggered by the prompting figure (e.g., implications of sexuality and labour embedded in fig cultivation). The logic of association obtained by means of resemblance (deeply lobed fig leaves are shaped like human genitalia?), contiguity (fig leaves were the closest thing available?), or stimulus-response (eat the fruit of flesh and see what response you get?) overlooks this intervention of configurative arrangements in all fragments of sign processing.

RETICLES WITHOUT "ARBORESSENCE"

Properties of networking bring us back to a "theoreticle" approach to the nervous sign process. The reticular imagery (a network of sign cells binding and supporting the nervous sign tissue) points to theories of rhizomatic growth. A rhizome is a system of tubercles, bulbs, and nodules endowed with a multitude of rootlets and radicles that grow under or along the ground, ordinarily in a horizontal position. Neurons follow similar patterns of growth known as "arborization," the bushy arrangement of dendrites around adjacent nerve cells. Note that in the language of Deleuze and Guattari (1987), the underworld rhizome differs radically from all "arborescent models," tree-like formations that may take different shapes or structures. Arborescent models include genealogical interpretations of human behaviour and history, accounts of social events based on their root origins and perceptible offshoots (e.g., looking for seeds of capitalism in the rise of Protestant ethics). Arborescence also feeds into theories of genetic evolution and the Code, which emphasize the logic of binarism and divarication – structural dualities that pit economy against ideology, synchrony against diachrony, *la langue* against *la parole*. Last but not least, arborescence is wedded to the search for the essence, the first principles and the foundations of forms of social life (e.g., the law of value that governs the logic of capital, in a Marxist perspective).

Arborescent thinking is hierarchically structured and geared to the pursuit of origins, foundations, first principles, essences,

and root forms of social and natural history. Tree-shaped models
of knowledge and history are premised on recursive applications of binary thinking, a principle that ties all branching
connections to main stems and genetic forms. They subordinate
signs of lower-level multiplicity to categories of higher-level
unity, reducing concrete twigs of history and language to offshoots of invariant stages and forms (Deleuze and Guattari
1987: 13–17, 27, 35ff., 46–8, 52; cf. Chevalier 1997: 4–19).

By contrast, rhizomatic growth is arborization without "arboressence." Rhizomatic formations are polymorphous and "incur-
rent," nothing like excurrent plants that have a straight, undivided main stem. But this is not to say that rhizomes escape all
forms of patterning. While antigenealogical, a rhizome is a
process in its own right, a web displaying warps and woofs
that follow certain regularities. Needless to say, the rhizome is
at home in semiosis. Sign processing is a method of doing things
in language and society. It generates the orderly "processes"
and "procedures" of language and social pragmatics, whether
naming practices, habits of family life, a narrative tradition, a
way of livelihood, a property system, or a mode of government.
Making sense of pragmatic sign activity requires therefore that
we identify the procedures and ways of carrying on the business
of sign spinning and weaving. The exercise implies that we
explore dispositions or propensities to act in certain ways, the
manners of proceeding in culture and society, and the ensuing
regularities governing sign and social behaviour. These procedures cannot be reduced to unit acts or simple operations performed by single individuals, like consumer choices aggregated
into abstract models. Far from being the total sum of its con-
stituent elements, life in society is a reticulum, a "relational
totality" of lines and fields of confederate activity (cf. Giddens
1987: 80–7).

THE TRULY GENERAL

Whereas arborescent structures aspire to rise far above the soil
that gives them birth, rhizomes never leave the ground. These

reticles are nonetheless capable of giving shape to manifestations of high-level generality and the lower levels of the truly
singular alike. To begin with, the rule of connectivity applies
to the "truly general," including claims to universality, or the
single clamour of Being for all beings. The notion of Being in
Spanish captures this point. In it lies a plural motif pointing to
a division and relationship between essence (*"ser"*) and posi-
tionality in time and space (*"estar"*). Being is like "conception";
it both denies and signifies the birth of body in time. Other
languages may signify full unity in Being, yet measures of
creative composition are still required.

Principles of assemblage also preside over the broad-level
configurations of social life, including the weavings of complex
signs and institutions in modern history. Sign actions are interwoven into markets, states, churches, and sciences assembled
into modern lifeworld fabrics. This means that "utterances are
not part of ideology, there is no ideology; utterances, no less
than states of things, are components and cog-wheels in the
assemblage ... one is only assembling signs and bodies as heterogeneous components of the same machine" (Deleuze and
Parnet 1987: 71, cf. 112; see also Deleuze and Guattari 1987:
11, 18, 69). Sound-images intersect with other signs, words with
other meaningful actions, and inscriptions with fully developed
institutions. Literacy comes with commodity exchange, state
formation with capital accumulation, monogamy with Christianity, modern industry with science and technology, body
piercing with biotechnology and postmodernity (see *The 3-D
Mind* 2). Words, inscriptions, and institutions are so closely
interwoven that only social change can disentangle them.

Sign utterances combine with other inscriptive actions and
processes to form machines and regimes of social history. Art,
class struggle, scientific and religious events, public speeches,
eating habits, and judicial procedures all interlace in tissues that
vary in tightness and looseness, with threads being looped and
unlooped according to circumstance and history.[23] Social threads
that come together form patterns pointing to configurations of

micro- and macro-history. However complex and variable they may be, organizational forms of the modern era are shot through with common threads – for instance, the fabric of contractual rights and obligations that bind husbands and wives, wage-labourers and employers, citizens and government. Configurative arrangements that bring signs and actions together converge on what might be called a machinic assemblage, the "abstract line" that crosses various elements, fluxes, and intensities and makes them work together (Deleuze and Guattari 1987: 9–11). The machine in question is a regime of sign actions "defined by its lines, axes and gradients, a whole, separate machine functioning distinct from organic functions and from mechanical relationships" (Deleuze and Parnet 1987: 105; cf. 106–8, 113). In the same vein Derrida (1973: 132) defines an assemblage as the "structure of an interlacing, a weaving, or a web, which would allow the different threads and different lines of sense or force to separate again, as well as being ready to bind others together."

Confederations of differences are what sign regimes are made of (Deleuze 1994: 56). "The minimum real unit is not the word, the idea, the concept or the signifier, but the *assemblage* ... The utterance is the product of an assemblage – which is always collective, which brings into play within us and outside us populations, multiplicities, territories, becomings, affects, events" (Deleuze and Parnet 1987: 51). Though a totality in its own right, each assemblage is hooked up to other machines, connecting patterns to other patterns. That is, each assemblage is a working reticle, a partial network harnessed to other machines and assembly lines of individual and collective behaviour. It is "a multiplicity which is made up of many heterogeneous terms and which establishes liaisons, relations between them, across ages, sexes and reigns – different natures. Thus, the assemblage's only unity is that of co-functioning: it is a symbiosis, a 'sympathy'. It is never filiations which are important, but alliances, alloys; these are not successions, lines of descent, but contagions, epidemics, the wind" (ibid.: 69).

This line of reasoning applies to all forms of semiosis, including signs of cultural montage – syncretic arrangements of intersecting languages. As with culture, *la langue* is neither fixed nor homogeneous. It is not governed by fixed rules of competence and conventionality. It is certainly not ruled by universal invariants, fixed equations to which external factors can be added to account for variations in levels of performance and deviations from norms (Chomsky 1988: 115–16). Language and culture are not exercises in semiotic coherence. Sign activity is rather "a mix, a mixture of several regimes of signs ... The Hebrews straddle a nomadic semiotics, which they profoundly transform, and an imperial semiotics, which they dream of restoring on new foundations by reconstructing the Temple" (Deleuze and Parnet 1987: 113; for a discussion of the scriptures straddling apocalyptic semiotics and imperial astromythology, see Chevalier 1997). The authors go on to say that "there are therefore several languages in a language ... The point is not 'bilingual', 'multilingual'; the point is that every language is itself so bilingual, itself so multilingual, that one can stutter in one's language, be a foreigner in one's own language, that is, push ever further the points of deterritorialization of assemblages" (Deleuze and Parnet 1987: 116). In the end, "natives" are always foreigners to themselves. They too may attempt to "decode" their "own" language or culture and become "cryptanalysts" without leaving home (cf. Jakobson and Halle 1956: 17).

Culture and society viewed as montage or assemblage is a far cry from the Husserlian notion of a people united in spirit. The spirit in question is an immanent identity that puts a unifying stamp on all the cultural achievements of a particular family-like circle, for example, the modern-day European supranationality. Husserl may be critical of historians who wish to emulate the natural scientists, yet he proposes that we substitute a spiritual taxonomy for a zoology of peoples (Husserl 1965: 155–8). His notion of spiritual types is a concession to cultural essentialism. Elsewhere he offers a better insight into cultural history. He describes it as consisting of configurations "filled with all types of human beings and of cultures, but constantly *flowing into each other.* It is like a sea in which human beings, peoples, are the waves constantly forming, changing, and disappearing, some more richly, more complexly involved, others more simply" (1965: 156, my emphasis).

Notions of collective spirits contradict the tidings of cultural history. Should we conclude from this that identity politics (nationalism, radical feminism, biological-gay rhetoric) should be dismissed because founded on erroneous assumptions of fixed subjectivity? Not necessarily. As with other discourses, the merit of identity rhetoric lies not in its truth-value understood in a representational perspective, but rather in its power to reinforce or destabilize existing regimes. Critics of essentialism should bear in mind that fictions of (relative) homogeneity and stable foundations can feed into struggles for social change, using "strategic essentialism" to promote new social pragmatics and multiplicities otherwise repressed. All assemblages feed into existential problems, including those that are constructed through signs of selfsame identities and essential spirits.

THE TRULY SINGULAR

"Strategic essences" notwithstanding, a rhizomatic approach to sign pragmatics contradicts the rule of undivided identities operating at the level of the truly general. "Theoreticle" reasoning destablizes all coherent totalities of language, culture, and society predicated upon firm attributional boundaries fixed in time and space. But the same reasoning applies to the truly singular. Thus we have seen how denotations and proper names are generated through montage. Although apparently descriptive, proper names are no exception to the rule of sign reticulation. "There are no literal words" (Deleuze and Parnet 1987: 3), only constructions of literality. The same qualification may be extended to signs of the subject, an entity that owes its self-formation to the compositional devices of objects and subjects assembling *in the subject.* For instance, while my proper name is meant to signify a unique "subject," it also carries with it signs of "objective biology." As already explained, signs of maleness and the father's blood transmitted through "natural" means are "incorporated" into a signature otherwise purely mine (Jacques M. Chevalier). In the words of Nancy (1993: 11), "the subject contains its difference from itself. The subject not only has this difference, it *is* this difference."

According to Lyotard (1988: 35, 37–8, 46), denominative words, proper names, and anthroponyms are "simple deictic signs" that fix the referent prior to making ostensive descriptions and predications and expressing knowledge about it. Names emerge before the named reality shows and signifies itself through experience. The argument goes against all "theoreticle" reasoning. While it is true that the name Jacques M. Chevalier must show some stability from one phrase to another if it is to function as sign, it is not for all that "a pure mark of the designative function," an "empty and constant designator" that sets the scene for fully formed expressions of the representational apparatus (ibid.: 1988: 39, 43–4, 52). Stability and relative autonomy should not be confused with the simplicity of nominative essences and therefore independence from code and predication.

To be sure, all predications of the named subject *cannot* be derived from the subject's signature; names are not empowered to say where people live, let alone what they eat and when they die. All the same, some compositional information is built into personal names. Proper nouns evolve within broader webs of sign activity and are meaningful assemblages in their own right. The referent event, object, or person named and located within a nominative network is "feebly determined in terms of its sense by dint of the large number and of the heterogeneity of phrase universes in which it can take place," yet this does not mean that "sense (*Sinn*) and reference (*Bedeutung*) must always be distinguished" (Lyotard 1988: 50–1). Sign actions can be disassembled and reassembled in ways that are highly variable (within limits – a phrase equating the name Jacques M. Chevalier with an Aztec divinity is a most unlikely event!).

Label-like utterances that point to undivided subjects, legal persons, or person-like identities (a city, people, plant species, typhoon, company, public square, religion, etc.) are subject to all sorts of configurative arrangements. Proper naming entails an individuation process based upon a montage of meaningful terms and relations, hence "something which happens, at least between two terms which are not subjects" (Deleuze and Parnet 1987: 51, cf. 120). As with other nouns, proper names do not escape the informative *bricolage* of culture and language. Some proper name compositions happen (*Positiv* + *ism, Sad* + *ism, Parkinson* + *disease*) while others do not or are subject to the vagaries of social history – reasons that invite the questioning of signs. (Why did Modernism come about in the late nineteenth century?) In the end, nothing escapes the meaningful play of difference.

Reticular activity shapes the lower level of the truly singular, the unique self or individual, and all things deemed incomparable, as Deleuze (1994: 303–4) remarks. Constructions of self-singularity thus point to a self that is forever emerging and entangled, never to congeal in a solid, compact identity modelled on the self-centred "me, myself, and I." According to Guattari (1995: 65–6), observations of pre-verbal child psychology suggest "a psychical world where family characters do not yet constitute autonomised structural poles, but disclose ... multiple, dislocated and entangled, existential Territories and incorporeal Universes." The end result is "an autopoietic snowball which renders the development of the sense of self and the sense of the other totally interdependent ... The emergent self – atmospheric, pathic, fusional, transitivist – ignores the oppositions of subject-object, self-other and of course masculine-feminine." This emergent self "is not a phase, since it will persist in parallel with other self formations and will haunt the adult's poetic, amorous and oneiric experiences." Self-formation is never fully consummated.

Given that it dwells in language, the subject spells out a new birth and a stillbirth all in the same breath. The interlacing of sign activity thus thrives on the death of the subject. This is so true that a statement affirming that "I am" can make sense without knowledge of who it is exactly that "I" is meant to stand for. Contrary to claims of Husserlian phenomenology, my death is structurally necessary to the pronouncing of the *I* ... The statement "I am alive" is accompanied by my being dead, and its possibility requires the possibility that I be dead ... The anonymity of the written *I*, the impropriety of the *I am writing*, is, contrary to what Husserl says, the "normal situation." The autonomy of meaning with regard to intuitive cognition, what Husserl established and we earlier called the freedom or "candor" [*franc-parler*] of language, has its norm in writing and in the relationship with death. This writing cannot be added to speech because, from the moment speech awakens, this writing has duplicated it by animating it. Here indication neither degrades nor diverts expression; it dictates it (Derrida 1973: 96–7).

"Real objects" are subject to a similar fate: they too are denied the life of singular objects as soon as they are given a mean-ingful existence. The erasure of both the sign-making subject and the thing-made-sign is inherent to the process of significa-tion. Neither subjects nor objects exist in the singular, with stable lives of their own. Rather, their mission is to confederate, doing it in such multiple ways that they can be reproduced even in the absence of the things and thoughts they allegedly signify. Words to the effect that "I see a particular person by the win-dow" are intelligible even when far removed from the space and time of their "original" utterance. They produce pathway connections that do not hinge on the speaker's presence and the listener's perception or intuition of the original experience "indicated" by such words. "The absence of intuition – and therefore of the subject of the intuition – is not only tolerated by speech; it is required by the general structure of signification, when constituted in itself. It is radically requisite: the total absence of the subject and object of a statement – the death of the writer and/or disappearance of the objects he was able to describe – does not prevent a text from 'meaning' something." Since "writing" is "the common name for signs which function despite the total absence of the subject because of (beyond) his death," then we must conclude that "writing" is implicated in every act of signification, including living speech (Derrida 1973: 93). In writing and the death of the subject reside the playfulness of language and the constant possibility that freedom from the senses may be abused (as in "the dog meows at the sight of a skyhook"). Illogicality and fiction are action potentials inherent to semiosis (Jakobson 1985: 135).

TEMPTATIONS OF THE TREE
OF KNOWLEDGE

Reticular activity governs the truly general and the truly singular alike, thereby countering all aspirations to the logic of "arboressence." Yet the death of the speaking subject or the spoken object does not result in pure chaos. While it never imposes full unity, an assemblage requires some consistency. Even in a Derridean perspective, signs of *différance* will generate patterns and transformations that are amenable to scientific analysis and universal claims thereof (Derrida 1981a: 28). Signs are not pure events, empirical particulars that can never be reproduced. After all "a sign which would take place but 'once' would not be a sign; a purely idiomatic sign would not be a sign ... A phoneme or grapheme ... can function as a sign, and in general as language, only if a formal identity enables it to be issued again and to be recognized" (Derrida 1973: 50).

Sign activity thus presupposes a "plane of consistency," a force that introduces "style" into acts of heterogeneous potentialities (Deleuze and Parnet 1987: 2). The word "consistency" evokes the degree of solidity or liquidity that characterizes the overall density of something. Brain imagery is good material for this theory. Notwithstanding their organic divisions, brain convolutions have properties of softness and semiviscosity in common, a degree of consistency that holds the tissues together, as it were. Viewed semiotically, the notion of consistency points to an "abstract line" that can hold disparate actions and forces together. The plane of consistency governing a sign regime can be pictured as a "soft intelligence" that does not involve clearly divided members and organs of mental hardware – say, a language system coherently divided into phonetics, syntax, and semantics. This mushy intelligence acts rather like a living totality "dis-membering" itself and the social organism into convolutions of all sorts. It "thinks" like a living tissue traversed with nomadic fluxes and nervous intensities that constantly reticulate and rearticulate the body social, generating multiple scannings of its self (Deleuze and Guattari 1987: 10, 21ff., 60; Deleuze and Parnet 1987: 115–16, 118, 121). Lines of nervous intersections prevail here, which means that one set of social convolutions can always be excavated from beneath another (e.g., feudalism from beneath capitalism, or pagan astrology from beneath Christian prophecy). Lines and impulses moving in one gyrus take refuge in other convolutions equally mushy and nervous.

The counterpart of lines of consistency resides in lines drawn on the "plane of organization." The latter term refers to systems organized by way of code, function, and structure (e.g., specialized lobes in the brain, the logic and functions of capital), or stages developed by way of genesis, evolution, and finality (e.g., from feudalism to capitalism and then to socialism).[24] This is not a separate plane, however. The two planes are linked by means of complementarity. Since it maintains and allows a range of action potentials, the plane of consistency entails a capacity to both sustain and subvert the plane of organization. The consistency of capitalism may be one of considerable hardness (toughness for some, hardships for others), yet it is precisely by virtue of its hardness that the organism will exercise its capacity to reorganize, constantly corrupting itself for purposes of survival.

The twofold matrix developed in a Deleuzian perspective is "diagrammatic." The latter term introduces

a third component which is no longer simply generative or transformational, but *diagrammatic or pragmatic*. We must discover in every regime and every assemblage the specific value of the existing lines of flight ... And they are all this at once, they make at each moment a diagram, a map of what is blocked, overcoded, or, on the contrary, mutating, on the route to liberation, in the process of outlining a particular fragment for a plane of consistence. Diagrammatism consists in pushing a language to the plane where "immanent" variation no longer depends on a structure or development, but on the combination of mutating fluxes, on their productions of speed, on their combinations of particles (to the point where food particles, sexual particles, verbal particles, etc., reach their zone of proximity or indiscernibility: abstract machine) (Deleuze and Parnet 1987: 118f.; see also Deleuze and Guattari 1987: 59).

Chaos and logos, the orgiastic and the organic, are two sides of the same coin. The authors of *Mille Plateaux* and *Dialogues* thus concede that elements of structure and development, or hierarchy and despotism, are built from and into rhizomatic activity. Likewise, forces of chaos and fluidity are at work in tree-like systems of representation and social order.

The implication here is not that planes of organization are disassembled and reassembled with great frequency, in a way that each stage or form can be said to be stable, if only for a while. Diagrammatic theory does not suggest that organic systems exist but only in the form of arborescent structures that are inherently frail and short-lived. Diagrammatism is not a reformulation of the Lévi-Straussian theory of *bricolage* presided over by the kaleidoscopic mind. A rhizome is not to be confused with *la pensée sauvage* (the savage mind but also the wild pansy). It has little to do with structuralism's tubular box (the brain, the intellect) constantly rearranging its pebbles in orderly ways, generating well-organized patterns (a myth, a totemic classification system, etc.) soon to be dismantled by the motions of history – palaces forever swept away by the flood (Lévi-Strauss 1966: 36, 232). Against this view, students of rhizomatic activity should consider the interdependence that lies between the two planes, over and beyond their opposition in logic or succession in time. Organizational order can be found in the plane of consistency, through patterns and pathways of reticular activity. But the argument goes in the other direction as well. That is, the plane of organization contains "chaosmotic" and fractal properties of its own. For reasons yet to be examined, order thrives on the vital forces of chaos.

But this is an issue to be explored later, in *The 3-D Mind 2*. Suffice it to suggest for the moment that it is one thing to say that organizational order and structure is ephemeral and will never last, a structural thesis *par excellence*, and another to say that the looseness of forces deviating from pivotal lines is vital to semiosis, something essential to the "plane of organization." The latter position is central to my essays in neurosemiotics – the notion that looseness and breaches of "law and order" are part and parcel of the nervous sign process and related pragmatics and regimes of social life. Transgression links up with norm and structure in many odd ways.

The planes of consistency ("mapping") and organization ("modelling") are not easily disentangled. They are so intertwined that contrasts between the two will not do justice to their interweavings. This means that our "theoreticle" paradigm should not present itself as just another "tree of knowledge," one that happens to be neatly divided into two sets of ramifications: namely, well-ordered branches and bushy rhizomes. The tree in question is perhaps original in that it grows upside down, with rhizomes "rising above" the branches in the sense of deserving greater attention. In rhizomatic theory, forces of arborization are elevated above principles of arborescence. Deleuzian theory emphasizes the rhizomatic aspects of sign processing, or the gaps and fluxes characteristic of the plane of consistency. Yet equal attention goes to the divarication of two planes. Paradoxically, a thesis opposing branches and bushes contradicts the critique of binarism built into the main argument. The logic of divarication ends up being essential to a theory that purports to elevate rhizomatic differences above the binarism of arboreal and genealogical thinking. Like wars that never stop, one antagonism aspires to put an end to all attacks of contagious dualism.

In reality, postmodern philosophy is not a "frank" plea for the erratic and the chaotic. Nor is it a dialectical account of sign and social history featuring the embattlement of *two poles of equal force*: the fractal versus the organizational, the rhizomatic versus the arborescent, or tropical jungles versus the gardens of Versailles. Postmodern rhetoric is rather a "machinic assemblage" of forces of dominance and lines of supplementation. Though often criticized in Derridean and Deleuzian theory, the plane of organization is given a crucial role of supplementation that feeds into the polemics of one principle lording it over another. Through supplementation, one rule (rhizomatic) is set against and elevated above another (arborescent) but without eliminating it. Concessions of "functional hierarchies" attenuate the rigidities of theoretical binarism. We have seen that similar operations apply to mundane imageries that bring planes of convergence and divergence together. In this sense, theoretical discourse does not differ from other assemblages of semiosis. Despite their claims to philosophical status, rhizomes can be suspected of growing in the same fields as corn, fig trees, and hemlocks.

Talk about lines and forces moving on a thousand plateaux would exercise little attraction were it not for its vertical arrangement of sign coordinates appearing in the guise of a Janus-faced "rhizomatic plane of organization." Tactics of attentional stratification and rank order – the subject matter of *The 3-D Mind 2* – generate a theoretical plan that stresses nomadic distributions organized into "crowned anarchies" (Deleuze 1994: 37). All indications are that this "planning of signs" is but an instance of "sign plotting." The king may be dead. Still, long live the king.

The Nervous Line

Given my "rank order" thesis, the question is whether we can construct a middle-of-the-road paradigm that can truly maintain the delicate balance between nomadic distributions and the strictures of the plane of organization. Is there a "milieu" or "middleness" that will allow the forces of convergence and divergence to intersect, without one principle ruling out or ruling over the other? Can the inequities of logical colonialism and heteronomy be effectively avoided (Jakobson 1985: 129–30)? Can diacritic and syncretic principles interact in ways that preclude the simplicities of binary reasoning and all related "stopgap" exercises – middlemost fillings couched in the language of structural or dialectical mediation?

These questions take us back to basic issues regarding the weavings of sign activity. One "flexible simple" that may help us in formulating an option developed right "in the middle" is that of a synaptic "line" binding one sign action to another. The threadlike mark should be conceived as both an empty space that divides and a copula that connects. A closely related imagery is that of mathematical bar combining two inherent properties. On the one hand, the bar is inherently fractional, dividing one quantity or value from another. On the other hand, the same bar is by necessity relational. The line breaks up the world into separate variables and yet connects them within variable equations. This twofold bar is eminently semiotic. It acts as a relational and fractional measure that hooks up one meaningful act or composition to another, allowing

"structural copulation" between signifiers – not between signifiers, signifieds, and referents (Baudrillard 1990: 161). The bar
thus occupies the synaptic space that resides between signs such
that no "s" (for sign) can exist as the Latin "*esse*" standing for
a self-sufficient "essence." One sign makes sense only when
affecting and affected by other signs. "Signaptic" actions and
reticles are produced and evolve within webs of sign events
assembled into semiotic machines.

As in Kantian philosophy, meaning requires the introduction
of "mathematics" into experience, measurements that bring
signs of "integral" and "differential" calculus – syncretic and
diacritic operations – to bear on the phenomenal world. The
implication is that phenomena can never be "things knowable
in themselves." No "object of sense" can be liberated from the
formal conditions of our sensibility, which include the application of the mathematics of "extensive quantities" to all objects
of experience (Kant 1984: 133, cf. 110). By extensive quantities
Kant means that which force whole objects to be represented
with prior reference to an aggregation of its component parts.
Thus a line exists by virtue of points and coordinates marking
its limits and divisibility within space. "All phenomena are,
accordingly, to be considered as aggregates, that is, as a collec-
tion of previously given parts" (ibid.: 132, my emphasis). We
have seen how the same language can be applied to sign reticles.
Like Kant's *quanti*, they are "empirical compositions of the
homogeneous" and "synthetical unities of the sensuous manifold" (ibid.: 131). Measurements of the self and the subject are
also subject to these mathematical rules. The self is derived
from a conjunction of the manifold representations considered
to be singularly "mine." Here again "the category of unity
presupposes conjunction" (ibid.: 94–6).

Unlike Kant's *quanti*, however, sign measurements are neither
constant nor universal. Also, they are indistinguishable from
physical experience – from complex actions of neurological,
biological, and chemical calculus. The sign *quanti* presented
throughout this book do not lend themselves to the Kantian
pursuit of abstract universals and categorical imperatives. They

do not converge on a mental apparatus that constitutes phenomena of the senses and determines all experience of the phenomenal world. Sign patterns and assemblages are not a priori
categories of sensuous intuition that make our experience of
objects possible. Kant insists that "we cannot think any object
except by means of the categories" (ibid.: 111). In his view,
"all sensuous intuitions are subject to the categories, as conditions under which alone the manifold content of them can be
united in one consciousness" (ibid.: 100). A priori categories
that have their origin in the understanding alone, independently
of sensibility, make it possible for all the manifold given in an
intuition to transcend the sensible and acquire conceptual unity
and objective validity (ibid.: 111).

Our discussion of sign reticulation departs from Kant's a
priori thinking. It also eschews the Kantian unity of objects
conceived by the mind. Although derived from the conjunction
of the manifold, Kant's categories of understanding applied to
objects and phenomena allow the manifold to be united in a
given intuition which requires unity of consciousness. "In order
to cognize something in space (*for example, a line*), I must draw
it, and thus produce synthetically a determined conjunction of
the given manifold, so that the unity of this act is at the same
time the unity of consciousness (in the conception of a line),
and by this means alone is an object (a determinate space)
cognized" (ibid.: 97, my emphasis). All the points of a line can
be drawn provided that the mind consciously sustains the idea
of a line throughout the action of drawing. Given this line of
reasoning, all indications are that Kantian "lines" are drawn
on the plane of convergence, in the direction of universal categories of consciousness transcending divisions and differences
of the sensuous and the manifold.

Sign mathematics cannot be reconciled with yet another tenet
of Kantian thought: the unity of self-consciousness achieved
through the transcendental subject. Kant claims that sensuous
unities conjoining the manifold presuppose the intuition or pure
analytical apperception of the self, as in the "I" of "I think"
or "I draw the line." The "I" points to the transcendental and

universal character of self-consciousness. It constitutes a necessary condition for the manifold representations to be conjoined
synthetically as "my" representations. The "I" exists by virtue
of this self-consciousness of the synthesis of "my" representations – "my" points of a line. It conjoins a host of categorical
applications otherwise fragmented in the scattering of empirical
consciousness. "I am, therefore, conscious of my identical self,
in relation to all the variety of representations given to me in
an intuition, because I call all of them my representations. In
other words, I am conscious myself of a necessary *a priori*
synthesis of my representations, which is called the original
synthetical unity of apperception, under which rank all the
representations presented to me, but that only by means of a
synthesis" (ibid.: 96).

In Kantian philosophy, synthesis wins over syncresis. Logical
as they may be, the mathematics of semiosis do not require the
Kantian unity of objects and subjects, let alone the synthetic
unity of categories bridging the gap between mind and world.
The "extensive quantities" of sign action potentials point
instead to lines and reticles in flight, a multiplicity of intensities
and confederate forces moving in multiple directions. Sign reticles are not unitary, well-ordered, finite structures that operate
independently of one another and that must be reconstructed
via categorical tree-like diagrams. Rather, they form webs of
intersecting lines simultaneously overlapping and fleeing, vectors and forces competing for attention and unevenly covered
with fragments and blank spaces, arrivals and departures, losses
and digressions. The interweavings of sign activity are so malleable and adaptable that they can divide and conquer the
manifold of social life. In the final analysis, sexuality and eth-
nobotany, verbal utterances and body language, inscriptions
and institutions, kinship and law, markets and churches, urban
spaces and architectural designs, technology and landscape all
are amenable to the manifold *quanti* of nervous sign processing.

Notes

1 Ears show weaker signs of hemispheric dominance.
2 It is assumed that while a stimulus fed into one ear will be processed by both hemispheres, competing stimuli presented simultaneously will proceed mostly through contralateral pathways. Correlatively, information transmitted through smaller ipsilateral pathways will be blocked.
3 While normal subjects are more skilful at doing puzzles with their left hands (RH), split-brain patients show an even greater difference in right and left manual performances.
4 Split-brain subjects have difficulty using their LH to name scents presented to the right nostril (which directly connects to the RH). They are nonetheless able to identify the corresponding object with the left hand (Temple 1993: 71).
5 Deut. 28.18, Job 16.13, 20.14, Prov. 5.4, Jer. 9.15, Lam. 3.15ff., Ezek. 8.3ff., Hos. 10.4, Amos 6.12, Matt. 27.34, Acts 8.23, Heb. 3.12, Rev. 8.11.
6 Num. 20.5, Deut. 8.8, Judg. 9.11, 1 Sam. 31.12, 25.18, 1 Kings 4.25, 10.27, 2 Kings 20.7, 1 Chron. 12.40, 2 Chron. 1.15, Neh. 13.15, Isa. 38.21, Mic. 4.4, Hag. 2.19, Zech. 3.10.
7 Ps. 78.47, 105.33, Jer. 5.17, 8.13, 24.1–8, 29.17, Joel 1.7, Hos. 2.12, Joel 1.7, 1.12, Amos 4.9, Hab. 3.17f., Nah. 3.12, Matt., 21.19–21, Rev. 6.13.
8 The narrative material examined here is based on my own translation of García de León's Spanish version of the myth.
9 The semantic information embedded in signs of this Nahua myth was gathered by researching the lexical, colloquial, and

etymological effects conventionally assigned to them. Part of this information was obtained through ethnosemantic interviews carried out in Pajapan, the village where García de León originally collected the myth. Ethnolinguistic associations come mostly from denotations and connotations assigned to the words by my Pajapan informants or by García de León, the author of a short Gulf Nahua dictionary. To this material I add references to entries appearing in the classical Nahuatl dictionary compiled by Rémi Siméon, originally published in 1885. To avoid gratuitous connections, most of the etymological interpretations offered in this analysis are based on Siméon's dictionary which contains extensive information on word formation by agglutination. I should stress that the purpose of these excursions into classical Nahuatl is not to explain Gulf Nahua mythology through Aztec culture. Rather, my intention is to suggest that some of the themes explored through this myth may be variations on linguistic usages dating back to pre-Hispanic times. Finally, the implications of each and every sign were explored by looking at connections made explicit in other variants of the same myth or in other manifestations of Gulf Nahua culture, such as rituals, folklore, and popular beliefs. My interpretive reading of this reference myth also takes into account ethnographic observations concerning the practical usages, perceptions, and knowledge associated with signs deployed in the narrative (for example, how iguana snares are made and used). All of this information collected either by myself or by other anthropologists may be used to unpack narrative symbolism situated in its proper cultural context.

10 The relevance of the iguana egg motif is made explicit in another Gulf Nahua variant of the corn myth (collected by the author in 1987), which compares the corn child to a ball of dough, shaped like an egg and placed in an iguana nest in a tree.

11 The black iguana is locally known as *bauisbinti*. It is smaller than the green *baguetspalin* (or quauhcuetzpalin) and lays its eggs in tree holes. In Nahuatl, the cayman alligator is called acuetzpalin, the water-lizard.

12 The word *nagastanpepel* appears to be a combination of *nagaz* for ear, and *penaga*, to be naked, or *pepetlaua*, to strip (*nimopepeci* means "I undressed myself"). To the Aztecs, a person who has large or sharp, angular ears (nacace, *nacazue-yac* in Pajapan) is by definition a wise person. As should be expected, the corn child is without wisdom. He is without *nacaztia* ("ears sticking out" in Pajapan), honours, or power in that, unlike a tenacaz, he represents no one. Alternatively, the narrative may suggest that the corn ear is without hair, another sign of powerlessness and immaturity. The young plant is deprived of the silk-hair needed to carry pollen to each seed for fertilization. In lieu of having "rock-like hair on his ears" (nacatzontel), hence being proud and rebellious, the boy is punished and humiliated (*nacazana*). That is, his ears are mutilated, bent or cut (*nagaztegui*). As a result, the boy is unable to understand the words uttered by the iguanas, as if "hard of hearing" (nacaztepetla) or stone-deaf (nacatzatzatl, denoting a "sticky substance" in Pajapan). Still, "doubled ears" can be turned to advantage. The imagery can serve as a sign of sacrificial behaviour, as among the Aztecs (cf. González Torres 1985: 102).

13 *Tauiltia* is to set fire (*tai* in the case of a maize plot). On these ancient associations between redness, water, the alligator, and the east, see León-Portilla 1983: 111, 122.

14 When preceded by and pronounced separately from the privative prefix *a*, the word *migui* denotes immortality. When pronounced as one word, *amiqui* (*at* + *migui*) implies death from thirst.

15 *Içatok* is to be alive, and *içaçan* means early. The east is also where the full moon appears, a good time for sowing and cutting wood (Münch Galindo 1983: 157). According to León-Portilla (1983: 111, 114, 122), the west used to be viewed as not only the sun's house but also the land of the moon at sleep and of women in general. Classical Nahua expressions echoing the Gulf Nahua solar imagery are tonatiuh iaquian and tonatiuh iquiçayan. Similar expressions are used by the Nahuas of Puebla (Taggart 1983: 57).

16 Nor can this upland-father and lowland-son imagery cope
with problems originating from the "upper" north (*para ahko*)
or the "lower" south (*para tani*), directions associated with
winds that blow at different times of the year. In Spanish the
norte denotes the north but also a "cold wind" (*cecekehegat*)
or rainstorm coming from the Gulf coast. Gulf Nahua milpas
and villages can be protected from north winds issued from
the mouth of a mythical serpent by placing a cross at each
corner of the plot or the community (Trujillo Jáuregui et al.
1982: 8, 19; on pre-Hispanic connections between death and
the cold north, see León-Portilla 1983: 111, 122). As for the
suradas (*tonalehegat*), they are strong "sun-winds" that blow
from the south during the dry season. Destructive winds
(*yualehegat*) from the south also blow in August. Winds
that damage maize crops are a reminder that sun and water,
two vital ingredients of life, can be quite deadly. Unless flames
are put out to "rest" (*ceuia*) or protection is found in the
shade (*gan ta ceui*), the sun can cause creatures to die of
heat (*tonalmigui*). Water without light and warmth can be
equally lethal. Rain and dew (*cekti*) are inherently cold
(*cecec*); they may freeze into ice (*cetl*), or they can turn into
cold water (*cecegat*) and fearsome storms descending from
the north.

17 The animal laughs at the red-haired *elote* boy, making him go
red and blush to the roots of his hair. It is as if the redness of
the dawning sun were turned against our inexperienced hero.
Pinahtia means to grimace, to humiliate or blame; the word
is from *pinah*, to be ashamed, to go red in the face, to be
saddened (also tlauia).

18 See Deleuze 1994: 37; Deleuze and Guattari 1987: 63; Deleuze
and Parnet 1987: 68; Massumi, in Deleuze and Guattari 1987:
xi-xiii, xvii.

19 See Massumi, in Deleuze and Guattari 1987: xiv; Deleuze 1994:
57, 295, 299; Guattari 1995: 73; Derrida 1973: 143.

20 See Deleuze 1994: 29f., 44f., 48, 58, 116, 262–8, 288.

21 See Deleuze and Guattari 1987: 16, 35ff., 60; Deleuze and
Parnet 1987: 111; Bourdieu 1990: 77f.

22 See Deleuze and Guattari 1987: 18; Deleuze and Parnet 1987: 111, 122.

23 See Deleuze and Guattari 1987: xiv, xvii, 48, 60; Deleuze and Parnet 1987: 118, 122.

Bibliography

Ashbrook, James B. 1988. *The Brain and Belief: Faith in Light of Brain Research*. Bristol, Ind.: Wyndham Hall.

Ayer, Alfred. 1967 [c.1936]. *Language, Truth, and Logic*. London: V. Gollancz.

Banich, Marie T. 1995. "Interhemispheric Processing: Theoretical Considerations and Empirical Approaches." In *Brain Asymmetry*, ed. Richard J. Davidson and Kenneth Hugdahl, 427–50. London: Bradford; Cambridge, Mass.: MIT Press.

Barlow, Horace. 1972. "Single Units and Sensations: A Neuron Doctrine for Perceptual Physiology?" *Perception* 1: 371–94.

Barthes, Roland. 1970. *S/Z*. Paris: Seuil.

Baudrillard, Jean. 1981. *For a Critique of the Political Economy of the Sign*. Transl. Charles Levin. St. Louis, Mo.: Telos.

– 1990. *Cool Memories*. Transl. Chris Turner. New York: Verso.

Blanco Rosas, José Luis. 1992. "Tierra ritual y resistencia entre los popolucas de Soteapan." In *Agraristas y agrarismo*, ed. Olivia Dominguez Pérez, 270–304. Xalapa, Mexico: Gobierno del Estado de Veracruz.

Boliek, Carol A., and John E. Obrzut. 1995. "Perceptual Laterality in Developmental Learning Disabilities." In *Brain Asymmetry*, ed. Richard J. Davidson and Kenneth Hugdahl, 637–58. London: Bradford; Cambridge, Mass.: MIT Press.

Bourdieu, Pierre. 1990. *In Other Words: Essays towards a Reflexive Sociology*. Transl. M. Adamson. Stanford: Stanford University Press.

Brown, Halle D., and Stephen M. Kosslyn. 1995. "Hemispheric Differences in Visual Object Processing: Structural versus Allocation

Theories." In *Brain Asymmetry*, ed. Richard J. Davidson and Kenneth Hugdahl, 77–98. London: Bradford; Cambridge, Mass.: MIT Press.

Bruder, Gerard E. 1995. "Cerebral Laterality and Psychopathology: Perceptual and Event-Related Potential Asymmetries in Affective and Schizophrenic Disorders." In *Brain Asymmetry*, ed. Richard J. Davidson and Kenneth Hugdahl, 661–91. London: Bradford; Cambridge, Mass.: MIT Press.

Bryden, M.P. 1986. "Dichotic Listening Performance, Cognitive Ability and Cerebral Organization." *Canadian Journal of Psychology* 40: 445–56.

Chevalier, Jacques M. 1990. *Semiotics, Romanticism and the Scriptures*. Berlin: Mouton de Gruyter.

– 1997. *A Postmodern Revelation: Signs of Astrology and the Apocalypse*. Toronto: Toronto University Press; Frankfurt: Vervuert.

– 2002a. *The Corpus and the Cortex: The 3-D Mind. Vol. 2*. Montreal and Kingston: McGill-Queen's University Press.

– 2002b. *Scorpions and the Anatomy of Time: The 3-D Mind. Vol. 3*. Montreal and Kingston: McGill-Queen's University Press.

Chevalier, Jacques M., and Daniel Buckles. 1995. *A Land without Gods: Process Theory, Maldevelopment and the Mexican Nahuas*. London: Zed; Halifax: Fernwood.

Chomsky, Noam. 1988. *Language and Problems of Knowledge*. Cambridge, Mass., and London: MIT Press.

Churchland, Patricia. 1986. *Neurophilosophy: Toward a Unified Science of the Mind/Brain*. London: Bradford; Cambridge, Mass.: MIT Press.

Davidson, Richard J. 1995. "Cerebral Asymmetry, Emotion, and Affective Style." In *Brain Asymmetry*, ed. Richard J. Davidson and Kenneth Hugdahl, 361–87. London: Bradford; Cambridge, Mass.: MIT Press.

Deleuze, Gilles, 1988. *Spinoza: Practical Philosophy*. Transl. Robert Hurley. San Francisco: City Light.

– 1994. *Difference and Repetition*. Transl. Paul Patton. New York: Columbia University Press.

Deleuze, Gilles, and Félix Guattari. 1987. *A Thousand Plateaus: Capitalism and Schizophrenia*. Transl. Brian Massumi. Minneapolis: University of Minnesota Press.

– 1994. *What is Philosophy?* Transl. Hugh Tomlinson and Graham Burchell. New York: Columbia University Press.

Deleuze, Gilles, and Claire Parnet. 1987. *Dialogues.* Transl. Hugh Tomlinson and Barbara Habberjam. New York: Columbia University Press.

Derrida, Jacques. 1973. *Speech and Phenomenon, and Other Essays on Husserl's Theory of Signs.* Transl. David B. Allison. Evanston: Northwestern University Press.

– 1981a. *Positions.* Transl. Alan Bass. Chicago: University of Chicago Press.

– 1981b. *Dissemination.* Transl. Barbara Johnson. Chicago: University of Chicago Press.

– 1982. *Margins of Philosophy.* Transl. Alan Bass. Chicago: University of Chicago Press.

Dumont, Louis, 1980. *Homo Hierarchicus: The Caste System and Its Implications.* Transl. Mark Sainsbury, Levis Dumont, and Basia Gulati. Chicago: University of Chicago Press.

Gadamer, Hans-Georg. 1994. *Truth and Method.* Transl. J. Weinsheimer and D. G. Marshall. New York: Continuum.

García de León, Antonio. 1966. "Semana Santa en Zaragoza, Veracruz." Unpublished manuscript.

– 1969. "El universo de lo sobrenatural entre los nahuas de Pajapan, Veracruz." *Estudios de cultura Nahuatl* 8: 279–311. México: UNAM.

– 1976. *Pajapan: Un dialecto Mexicano del Golfo.* México: Instituto Nacional de Antropología e Historia, Colección científica, no. 43.

– 1991. "Paraíso Perseguido." *Ojarasca* 2. México: Pro México Indígena.

Giddens, Anthony. 1987. *Social Theory and Modern Sociology.* Stanford: Stanford University Press.

Gonzáles Torres, Yolotl. 1985. *El sacrificio humano entre los Méxicas.* México: Instituto Nacional de Antropología e Historia.

Guattari, Félix. 1995. *Chaosmosis: An Ethico-Aesthetic Paradigm.* Transl. Paul Bains and Julian Pefanis. Bloomington and Indianapolis: Indiana University Press.

Harrington, Anne. 1995. "Unfinished Business: Models of Laterality in the Nineteenth Century." In *Brain Asymmetry,* ed. Richard J. Davidson and Kenneth Hugdahl, 3–28. London: Bradford; Cambridge, Mass.: MIT Press.

Hawthorne, Manning, and Henry W. Longfellow. 1947. *The Origin and Development of Longfellow's "Evangeline."* Portland: Anthoensen.

Heidegger, Martin. 1968. *What Is Called Thinking?* Transl. J. Glenn Gray. New York: Harper & Row.

Heilman, Kenneth M. 1995. "Attentional Asymmetries." In *Brain Asymmetry*, ed. Richard J. Davidson and Kenneth Hugdahl, 217–34. London: Bradford; Cambridge, Mass.: MIT Press.

Hellige, Joseph B. 1995. "Hemispheric Asymmetry for Components of Visual Information Processing." In *Brain Asymmetry*, ed. Richard J. Davidson and Kenneth Hugdahl, 99–121. London: Bradford; Cambridge, Mass.: MIT Press.

Hiscock, Merrill, and Marcel Kinsbourne. 1995. "Phylogeny and Ontogeny of Cerebral Lateralization." In *Brain Asymmetry*, ed. Richard J. Davidson and Kenneth Hugdahl, 535–78. London: Bradford; Cambridge, Mass.: MIT Press.

Hugdahl, Kenneth. 1995. "Classical Conditioning and Implicit Learning: The Right Hemisphere Hypothesis." In *Brain Asymmetry*, ed. Richard J. Davidson and Kenneth Hugdahl, 235–67. London: Bradford; Cambridge, Mass.: MIT Press.

– 1995. "Dichotic Listening: Probing Temporal Lobe Functional Integrity." In *Brain Asymmetry*, ed. Richard J. Davidson and Kenneth Hugdahl, 123–56. London: Bradford; Cambridge, Mass.: MIT Press.

Husserl, Edmund. 1965. *Phenomenology and the Crisis of Philosophy.* Transl. Quentin Lauer. New York: Harper & Row.

Hynd, George W., Richard Marshall, Josh Hall, and Jane Edmonds. 1995. "Learning Disabilities: Neuroanatomic Asymmetries." In *Brain Asymmetry*, ed. Richard J. Davidson and Kenneth Hugdahl, 617–35. London: Bradford; Cambridge, Mass.: MIT Press.

Iaccino, James F. 1993. *Left Brain–Right Brain Differences: Inquiries, Evidence, and New Approaches.* Hillsdale, N.J.: Lawrence Erlbaum.

Jakobson, Roman. 1985. *Selected Writings.* Vol. 7, *Contributions to Comparative Mythology: Studies in Linguistics and Philology, 1972–1982.* Ed. Stephen Rudy. Berlin: Mouton.

Jakobson, Roman, and Morris Halle. 1956. *Fundamentals of Language.* The Hague: Mouton.

Kant, Immanuel. 1984. *Critique of Pure Reason.* Transl. by J.M.D. Meiklejohn. London and Melbourne: Dent.

Kinsbourne, Marcel, and Merrill Hiscock. 1983. "The Normal and Deviant Development of Functional Lateralization of the Brain." In *Handbook of Child Psychology*, ed. P. Mussen. Vol. 2, *Infancy and Developmental Psychobiology*, ed. Marshall Haith and Joseph Campos, 157–280. New York: John Wiley & Sons.

León-Portilla, Miguel. 1983. *La filosofía nahuatl estudiada en sus fuentes*. México: UNAM.

Lévi-Strauss, Claude. 1962. *La pensée sauvage*. Paris: Plon.

– 1963a. *Structural Anthropology*. Transl. Claire Jacobson and Brooke G. Schoep. New York: Basic Books.

– 1963b. *Totemism*. Transl. Rodney Needham. Boston: Beacon Press.

– 1966. *The Savage Mind*. Chicago: University of Chicago Press.

– 1969. *Elementary Structures of Kinship*. Transl. James H. Bell, John Richard von Sturmer, and Rodney Needham. Boston: Beacon Press.

– 1987. *Anthropology and Myth, Lectures 1951–1982*. Transl. Roy Willis. Oxford: Blackwell.

Levy, Jerre. 1974. "Cerebral Asymmetries as Manifested in Split-Brain Man." In *Hemispheric Disconnection and Cerebral Function*, ed. Marcel Kinsbourne and W. Lynne Smith. Springfield, Ill.: C.C. Thomas.

Liotti, Mario, and Don M. Tucker. 1995. "Emotion in Asymmetric Corticolimbic Networks." In *Brain Asymmetry*, ed. Richard J. Davidson and Kenneth Hugdahl, 389–424. London: Bradford; Cambridge, Mass.: MIT Press.

López Arias, Marcelino. 1983. "El espíritu del maíz." In *El espíritu del maíz y otros relatos zoque-popolucas*. Acayucan: Dirección General de Culturas Populares.

Lyotard, Jean-François. 1988. *The Differend: Phrases in Dispute*. Transl. Georges Van Den Abbeele. Minneapolis: University of Minnesota Press.

Marieb, Elaine. 1993. *Anatomie et physiologie humaines*. Transl. Jean-Pierre Artigau, Sylvie Chapleau, Marie-Claude Désorcy, and Jean-Luc Riendeau. Québec: Renouveau Pédagogique.

Münch Galindo, Guido. 1983. *Etnología del Istmo Veracruzano*. México: UNAM.

Merleau-Ponty, Maurice. 1962. *Phenomenology of Perception*. Transl. Colin Smith. London: Routledge.

Nancy, Jean-Luc. 1993. *The Birth to Presence*. Transl. Brian Holmes and others. Stanford: Stanford University Press.

Orstein, Robert Evans. 1977. *The Psychology of Consciousness*. New York: Harcourt.

Peters, Michael. 1995. "Handedness and Its Relation to Other Indices of Cerebral Lateralization." In *Brain Asymmetry*, ed. Richard J. Davidson and Kenneth Hugdahl, 183–214. London: Bradford; Cambridge, Mass.: MIT Press.

Plato. *Cratylus*. Transl. Benjamin Jowett. Gutenberg etext.

Rosenzweig, Mark R., Arnold L. Leiman, and S. Marc Breedlove. 1999. *Biological Psychology: An Introduction to Behavioral, Cognitive, and Clinical Neuroscience*. Sunderland, Mass.: Sinauer.

Saussure, Ferdinand de. 1966. *Course in General Linguistics*. Ed. Charles Bally and Albert Sechehaye; transl. Wade Baskin. New York: McGraw-Hill.

Sergent, Justine. 1995. "Hemispheric Contribution to Face Processing: Patterns of Convergence and Divergence." In *Brain Asymmetry*, ed. Richard J. Davidson and Kenneth Hugdahl, 157–81. London: Bradford; Cambridge, Mass.: MIT Press.

Siméon, Rémi. 1977. *Diccionario de la lengua Nahuatl o Mexicana*. Transl. J. Oliva de Coll. México. México: Siglo Veintiuno.

Sundsten, John W. *The Digital Anatomist: Interactive Brain Atlas*. Seattle: University of Washington, 1994.

Taggart, James M. 1983. *Nahuat Myth and Social Structure*. Austin: University of Texas Press.

Temple, Christine. 1993. *The Brain*. London: Penguin Books.

Trujillo Jáuregui, Saturnino et al. 1982. *Rituales y creencias Nahuas*. Acayucan, Mexico: Dirección General de Culturas Populares.

Wittling, Werner. 1995. "Brain Asymmetry in the Control of Autonomic-Physiologic Activity." In *Brain Asymmetry*, ed. Richard J. Davidson and Kenneth Hugdahl, 305–57. London: Bradford; Cambridge, Mass.: MIT Press.

Zaidel, Eran. 1983. "Disconnection Syndrome as a Model for Laterality Effects in the Normal Brain." In *Cerebral Hemisphere Asymmetry: Method, Theory, and Application*, ed. J.B. Hellige, 95–151. New York: Praeger.

Index

extinction, and right-brain
attention, 29, 51
extrapersonal space, right-brain,
40

face recognition: bihemispheric,
43–4, 48, 53, 76, 81; left-
brain, 30; right-brain, 34–5;
split-brain, 41, 48
facial expression: hemispheric
differences, 63; right-brain
recognition, 78
Fall imagery, 103, 112–14, 116,
118–19, 120–1, 123
feminism: and binarism, 152;
on identity, 163; on representation, 141
fig imagery, 93, 114–24, 133,
157–8
fractals: and chaos, 7, 16, 154,
169–70; cultural, 10, 14
frontal lobe, 9, 28, 51, 63, 68.
See also coronal plane

Gadamer, Hans-Georg, 17, 19
Gall, Franz Joseph, 68. See also
phrenology
genealogy, arborescent, 158–9,
170
gestalt: background, 52–3, 72,
76, 78; right-brain, 25, 32–5,
41, 55, 66; split-brain, 44;
and supplementary opposi-
tion, 93, 110
grammatology, Derrida on, 20,
149
grandmother cell hypothesis, 91

Guattari, Félix. See Deleuze
et al.

Habermas, Jürgen, on instru-
mental reason, 9
habituation, right-brain, 51
Heidegger, Martin: on naming,
97; on time, 9
hemlock imagery, 103–5, 109,
123–5
Heraclitus: in Cratylus, 10,
13–14, 16; and essentialism,
7
hermeneutics, and narration, 6,
9
hexameter, 104–12
Hugdahl, Kenneth: on hemispheric bipolarity, 63, 77;
on right brain, 36, 41, 49;
on split-brain, 29
humour, right-brain, 35, 55
Husserl, Edmund: and cultural
essentialism, 162; Derrida on,
148, 150, 165–6; on science,
18

identity: cultural, 4; fixed, 145,
167; and harmony, 104; politics, 141, 163; proper name,
95, 97–8, 100, 102, 125,
127, 164–5; representational,
153, 175; and similarity, 34,
78
impulse: sign, 102, 118–9, 156,
168; synaptic, 86–9. See also
potential
indifference, left-brain, 63–4

interhemispheric: diacritic and syncretic complementarity, 77-81, 85, 108; noise, 59–60; suppplementation, 41, 49, 52, 78, 80, 85, 90, 93, 110, 113, 133, 171; whole brain activity, 38–48, 51–3, 56, 65–6, 70–1

ipsilateral pathways, 47–9, 51

Jackson, John H., on whole brain activity, 71

Jakobson, Roman: on decoding, 162; on diacritic mark, 79; on heteronomy, 172; on sign illogicality, 167; on sign relations, 148–9; and transdisciplinarity, 16–17; on writing, 148

Kant, Immanuel: on empirical knowledge, 58; on extensive quantities, 173–5

Lamb slain imagery, 80, 146

language: left-brain, 25–6, 33, 37–42, 45–50, 52, 62, 76–7; right-brain, 40–1, 61–2, 65, 76

lateralization: early, 46

LeDoux, Joseph, on emotional brain, 9

left-handedness: and attentional bias, 50; and autism and dyslexia, 29; and language, 27; and left-brain dominance, 26; and reading

disabilities, 33; and simultaneous matchings, 33

Lévi-Strauss, Claude: on code, 127; on cooking, 144; on name totem, 99; on origin, 145; on savage mind, 169; on similarities and differences, 77; on totemic mediation, 152

literacy: and commodity, 160; phonocentric, 69, 148, 150; and sign representation, 142

literality: left-brain, 55; proper name, 92, 94, 99, 163; use-value, 142, 144. *See also* denotation

lobes, 45

logocentrism: and cognitivism, 74–5; and representation, 151

Longfellow. *See Evangeline*

Luria, Alexander R., 16

Lyotard, Jean-François: on postmodern theory, 15; on proper names, 164

Marxism: on cultural misrepresentation, 139, 141–2; and dualism, 152; and essentialism, 158

mathematics: integral and differential, 81, 137, 173; Kantian, 173–5; left-brain, 26, 46, 52, 58, 69, 77; and metaphysics, 19–20; sign, 137, 172–5

mediation: competitive, 129, 132–3; dialectical, 138,